BRETHREN NEW TESTAMENT COMMENTARY

1 & 2 THESSALONIANS

Author, Timothy P. Harvey
General Editor, Harold S. Martin

BRF
Published by
Brethren Revival Fellowship
Ephrata, Pennsylvania

ISBN: 0-9745027-7-4

Unless otherwise noted, all Scripture quotations are from the
New King James Version, copyright 1990 by Thomas Nelson, Inc.

Copies of this book are available from:
Brethren Revival Fellowship
P. O. Box 543
Ephrata, PA 17522

GENERAL PREFACE

This commentary is part of a new series of studies that will feature a number of volumes covering all of the New Testament books. There will be reliable expositions of the Bible text, a careful analysis of key words, easy outlines to follow, and helpful material to aid serious Bible students. The explanations are written from a conservative evangelical Brethren and Anabaptist point of view. The goal is to expound the Bible text accurately, and to produce a readable explanation of God's truth.

Each volume can be especially useful for pastors, Sunday School teachers, and lay persons. The writers aim for thoroughness, clarity, and loyalty to the Anabaptist/Pietist values. The meaning of the Greek text (both for those who know Greek and those who don't), will be part of the exposition when necessary.

The *Brethren New Testament Commentary* sponsored by Brethren Revival Fellowship, will simply take the biblical text as it is, and give the exposition along with applications for everyday life. All who have been asked to write the commentaries in this series agree that the message of God's Word in its original documents was given without error, and that nothing more is necessary for spiritual growth.

Brethren Revival Fellowship is a renewal movement within the *Church of the Brethren* which aims to proclaim and preserve biblical values for living today. We believe the Bible is the infallible Word of God, the final authority for belief and practice, and that to personally accept Jesus Christ as Savior is the only means of salvation.

The Brethren Revival Fellowship Committee

This book is dedicated to my wife,
Lynette.
Your dedication to our family
and willingness to give your time and talent
to build a Christian home
are an inspiration and source of strength to me.

Many women do noble things, but you surpass them all...
a woman who fears the LORD is to be praised.
(Proverbs 31:29-30, NIV)

FOREWORD
The Books of 1 and 2 Thessalonians

Living with authenticity, struggling with difficult times, questionable sexual morals, confusion about the return of Christ, getting along with difficult people, faithful living in a complex age—this list of topics could come from any number of contemporary sources. Christians living in the 21st century face challenges like these every day. Issues such as these are found in newspapers, TV shows, and movies. They are found in families and churches. Every day, faithful believers are presented with opportunities for faithfulness or unfaithfulness. How is one to proceed?

Modern Christians are not the only ones to face difficult choices. The list of topics above, in fact, was not drawn at random from modern living; it was taken from the New Testament books of 1 and 2 Thessalonians!

The apostle Paul (along with his ministry partners Silvanus and Timothy) wrote these two epistles to the church they had planted in the city of Thessalonica. The epistles are intended to encourage a group of believers who were young in the faith, experiencing persecution, and yet finding much joy and success in their Christian life. In the midst of this faithful living, Paul also wanted to provide significant teaching on the return of Christ, and how believers should live in anticipation of that great event.

The book of 1 Thessalonians consists of Paul's words of encouragement and expression of love to this group of believers. It also contains a list of instructions concerning issues Timothy brought to Paul's attention after Timothy's return visit to Thessalonica. There is much practical material in this book which is directly relevant to issues faced by Christians today.

The book of 2 Thessalonians consists of further words of instruction to the Thessalonians. In the time between the writing of the two epistles, something has happened to bring confusion about the return of Christ into the young church at Thessalonica, and Paul writes to the church to get the believers there thinking "on the right track" again, as well as to provide further instruction.

Anabaptist and Pietist groups (like the Church of the Brethren and the Mennonite Church) have long been characterized by a "straight-forward" approach to interpreting the Scriptures. Such an approach insists that the faithful interpreter will accept what is written as authoritative, and seek to apply what is written to life. That is the approach followed in this commentary.

It has been a wonderful and challenging experience to write this commentary, and my prayer is that the material found here will be useful for sermon preparation, Sunday School teaching, and Bible study preparation. I also hope that it will be useful devotionally, and that Christians who are interested in the epistles of 1 and 2 Thessalonians will use this book along side their Bible, with the issues of their local congregation in mind.

A special word of thanks is extended to the Wednesday evening Bible study group at Central Church of the Brethren for engaging in honest study of these verses. This commentary is written out of that experience.

Tim Harvey
Central Church of the Brethren
416 Church Ave., SW
Roanoke, VA 24016

CONTENTS

FIRST THESSALONIANS

COMMENTARY
ON
1 THESSALONIANS

INTRODUCTION TO 1 THESSALONIANS

The first letter to the Thessalonians is a remarkably helpful letter for Christians living in the 21st century. Throughout this letter, Paul, Silvanus, and Timothy take truths of the gospel and apply them to situations that concerned regular, salt of the earth believers who called Thessalonica home in the years shortly following the death of Christ. A significant theme of 1 Thessalonians is *eschatology*, or the study of the end times. Indeed, Paul mentions Christ's return in each of 1 Thessalonians' five chapters, treating the topic at length in chapters four and five.

This commentary affirms that the end times is an important emphasis of this letter. It may be, however, that the overall theme of 1 Thessalonians is even more basic than that. An honest study of the letter leads one to conclude that Paul is concerned about *how to live faithfully to Jesus, knowing that He will return*. First Thessalonians does not deal with Jesus' return merely as a conversation piece, something to discuss for the sake of discussion. Instead, Paul instructs this young church *how they should live while they wait for Jesus*. Because Paul writes about a living faith, Christians—especially those from a believer's church background (Brethren, Mennonite and other Anabaptist and Pietist groups) will find this letter particularly relevant.

1. The background to the letter.

Before beginning the study of the letter itself, some background information will be helpful to "set the stage" for this study. Paul arrived in Thessalonica sometime in the years AD 49-52, on his second missionary journey (see Acts 15:39–18:22 for more detail on this journey). His traveling companions for this missionary work were Silvanus (or Silas) who was with Paul from the beginning of this trip (Acts 15:40), and Timothy, a young Christian whom Paul and Silas met in the city of Lystra (Acts 16:1).

The purpose of this missionary journey was to visit congregations that Paul had planted on his first missionary journey, but the three men also planted some new churches along the way. This was the case in Thessalonica, which is described in Acts 17:1-10. The three men arrived in the city and Paul, "as his custom was," began to preach in the local synagogue, proclaiming the good news of Christ's death and resurrection. The only reference to the length of time Paul spent in Thessalonica is in Acts 17:2, which says that Paul preached in the synagogue for "three Sabbaths." Judging by the amount of teaching and great depth of love shared between the apostles and the church, it seems that the three men spent more than just two weeks in Thessalonica from the overall strength and condition of the Thessalonian church.

Initially, the evangelistic effort was very successful, as "some of them were persuaded; and a great multitude of the devout Greeks, and not a few of the leading women, joined Paul and Silas" (Acts 17:4). This success, however, did not go unnoticed by the local Jewish leadership. These leaders "took some evil men from the marketplace" and caused such a commotion that Paul, Silas and Timothy had to escape Thessalonica by night, leaving the young congregation to fend for themselves. As is noted in 1 Thessalonians 3:2, some point Timothy returned to check on the Thessalonians, and found that they were doing quite well.

2. The city of Thessalonica

The city of Thessalonica was located on the northeast corner of modern-day Greece, known in Paul's day as Macedonia. In many ways, it was a typical Greek city of the day, filled with a whole host of gods, idols, and religions. One could worship the emperor cult of the Roman leadership, traditional Greek and Egyptian gods, or any of a number of "mystery religions," groups that claimed to have some special knowledge given to them by the "gods."

Economically and politically, Thessalonica was a thriving city. Because of its location along some major trade routes, the city enjoyed a fair amount of wealth through its abundant commerce. As capital of the province, the government of the city enjoyed special privileges from Rome. As capital city, people throughout the region naturally paid attention to what went on there. Therefore, Thessalonica was a strategic foothold for the gospel, as a thriving church in this city could have impact throughout the region.[1]

3. When and why Paul wrote this letter

It is most likely that Paul wrote this letter shortly after leaving Thessalonica. Acts 18:11 shows that Paul stayed in Corinth for a year and a half. It was during this extended ministry time in Corinth that Paul heard the encouraging report from Timothy and sat down with him and Silas to compose this letter.

Paul had several purposes in writing this letter. A brief outline shows that Paul praised the Thessalonians for their growth in the gospel (chapter 1); defended himself and encouraged the Thessalonians in the face of enemies (chapters 2 and 3); and provided some basic teaching concerning daily living (chapter 4), the return of Christ (chapters 4 and 5), and the order of the church (chapter 5). Throughout all of his

---

[1]   Michael W. Holmes, *1 & 2 Thessalonians, NIV Application Commentary,* page 18.

writing, however, Paul had one eye and ear toward heaven, anticipating Jesus' return at any moment.

4. A note about first century letter writing

When Paul wrote each of his epistles, he followed the standard letter writing format of the day. Much as our letter writing follows a standard form (date, salutation, some small talk, the body of the letter, and farewells) so the letters of that day followed a format similar to that of 1 Thessalonians.

The standard form of first century epistles and letters (with accompanying references to 1 Thessalonians) is as follows: a "prescript" identifying the senders (1:1a) and the recipients (1:1b); greeting (1:1c); prayer wish or thanksgiving (1:2-10); the body of the letter (2:1 – 5:22); and final greeting and farewell (5:23-28)[2]

A quick glance at the other New Testament epistles, as well as Acts 15:23-29, provides other examples of the standard letter form.

---

[2]   Gordon D. Fee and Douglas Stuart, *How to Read the Bible for All Its Worth,* page 46. Not all of Paul's letters contain each of the six parts, as is often true of our own letters today.

Chapter 1

SIGNS OF AUTHENTICITY
1 Thessalonians 1:1-10

Paul follows the standard letter writing format of his day in this epistle. The first chapter of the letter contains the prescript, the greeting, and the thanksgiving sections.

A study of these verses reveals both the great love Paul had for the Christians in Thessalonica, and the great enthusiasm he had for the work that God was doing in their lives. The Thessalonians displayed many traits of an authentic faith. Examining these traits and applying them to our lives is the task at hand.

1. Two signs of the authentic church (1:1)

Paul begins the epistle with a heartfelt blessing to the Thessalonian congregation.

(1:1) Paul, Silvanus, and Timothy, To the church of the Thessalonians in God the Father and the Lord Jesus Christ: Grace to you and peace from God our Father and the Lord Jesus Christ.

The position presented in this commentary is that the apostle Paul is the author of the epistle. This has been the testimony of the church through the ages. In the epistle, we see that Paul's name is first in the list of senders, and that he uses the pronoun "I" six times in the NKJV.

Even while affirming Paul as the author, it is apparent from studying the epistle that the thanksgiving and instruction found in the letter is the shared concern of Silvanus and Timothy as well. Their names occur in the prescript, and on several occasions Paul uses the pronouns "we" and "our" in his writing. Clearly, Silvanus and Timothy may be considered as "co-senders" of this epistle, and that the concerns and wishes for the church at Thessalonica penned by Paul are equally those of the other two men.

One might wonder about the conversation these three men had the night before Paul composed this epistle. Imagine sitting around the kitchen table or camp fire with these three giants of the early church: The apostle Paul, who combined the fire of an evangelist, the heart of a pastor, and the mind of a theologian; Silvanus (or Silas), who labored with Paul in his missionary work (Acts 15-18) and who would later end up in partnership with Peter (1 Peter 5:12); and young Timothy, the Spirit-gifted junior partner in the group, who later would become pastor of the congregation at Ephesus. What might one learn from "listening in" on this conversation? While the content of the letter is the result of their love and prayers for the church, two signs of the authentic church are suggested from the association these three men shared.

a. The authentic church values group discernment over private interpretation. Here is a simple illustration of three persons together seeking God's will for a particular congregation. Certainly Paul, Silvanus, and Timothy had many conversations and prayer sessions about the needs in Thessalonica. The epistle is the result of their sharing and prayer in the epistle.

Congregational discernment of the spirit of God is at the heart of Anabaptist and Pietist theology and practice. Many Christians believe that Bible study and inspiration from God are more than private matters. While many claim to "feel led" in a certain direction, those with a Pietist heritage (such as the Church of the Brethren) believe that in such instances the "inner word" (the inner testimony of the Holy Spirit) must be in harmony with the "outer word" (the testimony of

Scripture).[3] The church must reject inner leadings and private interpretations that contradict the clear teaching of Scripture. This commitment will help the church avoid much trouble as committed believers prayerfully work together to make sure those inner leadings are consistent with the written Word. The reverse must also be true.

b. *The authentic church is a body of believers held together by God, not a building held together by mortar.* If the church is going to understand God's will properly, then it must also properly understand what it means to be the church. Today, people talk about the church as a building where Christians meet once or twice on Sundays and on Wednesday evening. Often, people say they are "going to church," or invite their friends to "come to church." All of this talk about the church being a building at a certain location betrays an inaccurate understanding of what the church is. History has left no record of the mailing address of the Thessalonian church, and readers are none the worse for their ignorance. The point of the matter is that the building was not the church—the people were!

In the Greek language, Paul uses the word *ekklesia* to address the Thessalonians, which the NKJV translates as "church." It is a word that the people of Paul's day would have understood from local government. For people of Greek heritage, the *ekklesia* was the "public gathering of persons in the city to make decisions concerning appointments to official positions, changes in law, contracts, treaties,

---

[3] It was this commitment to both the "inner word" and "outer word" that caused the Schwarzenau Brethren to break with the Radical Pietists, and adopt practices of baptism, church discipline, Love Feast, and others. See Donald Durnbaugh, *Fruit of the Vine*, page 26. See also the article "Inner Word and Outer Word" in the *Brethren Encyclopedia*, page 656.

war and peace, and finance."[4] In its political usage, the idea would be similar to a New England town meeting, or even a denominational Annual Conference!

To help the Thessalonians understand their new Christian identity, Paul has taken a word that would have been quite familiar to the people and given it a new meaning. The *ekklesia* of the New Testament is the body of believers, gathered together to live as obedient followers of Jesus, the risen Savior. It makes no difference whether the people met together in the Temple courts (Acts 2:46), by a river (Acts 16:13), in the homes of believers, or in a church building. In Paul's mind, the importance of *ekklesia* was in what the people were doing, not where they were meeting. The old Brethren had it right when they called their buildings "meetinghouses."

Paul concludes the prescript of the letter by identifying the Thessalonians as a fellowship held together by God, by offering them the blessing of *grace* and *peace*. The Thessalonians have received *grace* as a gift of God the Father through the sacrificial death of Jesus Christ. It is grace that has changed them from objects of wrath to God's precious children, designed for good works in the kingdom of God. They have received *peace* through the assurance of that sacrificial work and the subsequent work of the Holy Spirit in their lives. All efforts for peace and reconciliation in the world must be based on the peace that only comes through the work of Jesus Christ and the forgiveness of sin.

Moving on from the "prescript" of the letter, Paul begins a prayer of thanksgiving for the faith that the Thessalonians are displaying. These words are a joyous outpouring

---

[4]   L. Coenen, "Church, Synagogue," *New International Dictionary of New Testament Theology, Volume I*, page 291.

of thanks for the good work and changed lives in the Thessalonian church. Paul's deep love for this congregation is unmistakable. We would do well to compose prayers of thanksgiving for our own congregations.

Paul's prayer of thanksgiving highlights several more qualities of authenticity, first of the individual believers (verses 2-4), then of the gospel that changed their lives (verses 5-8), and finally of conversion itself (verses 9-10).

2. Three signs of the authentic believer (1:2-4)

Paul begins his prayer of thanksgiving by relating their lives to the familiar New Testament triad of faith, love and hope.

(1:2-4) We give thanks to God always for you all, making mention of you in our prayers, remembering without ceasing your work of faith, labor of love, and patience of hope in our Lord Jesus Christ in the sight of our God and Father, knowing, beloved brethren, your election by God.

Here, and in seven other passages in the New Testament, (Romans 5, 1 Corinthians 13, Galatians 5, Colossians 1, 1 Thessalonians 5, Hebrews 10, and 1 Peter 1)[5] the three Christian qualities of faith, hope, and love appear together. If a person wanted to describe the Christian life in simple terms to someone who was asking about the faith, it would be quite appropriate to center the explanation on these three New Testament themes.

While the NKJV translates verse 3 quite literally, the NIV helpfully translates this phrase as "your work produced by faith, your labor prompted by love, and your endurance inspired by hope." The three signs of the authentic believers follow this translation.

---

[5] Jacob W. Elias, *1 & 2 Thessalonians*, *Believers Church Bible Commentary*, page 50.

a. Work produced by faith. "Work" and "labor" are typically seen as synonyms in the English language. An examination of their meanings in Greek, however, shows some difference in usage. Work is translated from the Greek *ergon*, and often simply means "work" as we would understand it from our daily lives. *Ergon* can also refer to the kind of work that brings achievement or accomplishes some good purpose.

This latter kind of work is what Paul thanks God for in the lives of the Thessalonians. It is a work produced by faith. New Testament faith is the assurance that God has acted decisively in Jesus to save people. It is the assurance that whatever trials and difficulties come, the powers of this world do not have the final say over our eternal destiny or even our day to day choices. We are saved by grace, through faith, and we live our lives as followers of Jesus Christ. Our "work of faith" is that which serves to advance the kingdom of God and brings glory to the name of Jesus.

Work here in no way suggests that we earn salvation through our own efforts. Yet it is true that a Christian cannot remain passive if spiritual growth is to occur. On this matter, Paul instructed the Ephesians to "put off, concerning your former conduct, the old man which grows corrupt according to the deceitful lusts, and be renewed in the spirit of your mind, and that you put on the new man which was created according to God, in true righteousness and holiness." (Ephesians 4:22-24). This is work in which we cooperate with God by involving ourselves in the spiritual disciplines of prayer, Bible study, worship, fasting, and giving. It is also work in which we authentically reflect Christ-like attitudes in our relations with the world as we share the gospel through word and deed. Such attitudes and practices will be addressed in greater detail in 1 Thessalonians 5:12-22.

b. Labor prompted by love. The Greek word *ergon* (translated "work") typically refers to that which brings some kind of achievement. But in the next phrase, the word *kopos* (translated "labor") is used. This word refers to work that comes as the result of some trouble or difficulty. *Kopos* is hard, labor-intensive work.

The unique quality of Jesus' love for us is that it is often like a fountain—it is most beautiful when there is an overflow. Our "labor of love" comes from an overflow of the sacrificial love of Jesus. First John 4:19 says that "we love Him because He first loved us." From this "overflow" of love, we work together in the church, whether it is disaster response, an evangelistic effort, a voluntary service assignment, or challenging social injustice. In challenging the principalities and powers of this age, we find that they will not go quietly. Laboring to bring the gospel into this world is hard work indeed.

Our labor of love must be for more than the program of the church. The church is not the building, and it is not the program. The church is the people. First John provides useful guidance here as well. Many places in that epistle remind us that if brothers or sisters claim to love God but hate their brother, these persons are liars. The fact is, our labor of love means loving our brothers and sisters, forgiving as appropriate, and seeing all the church family with the love of Jesus. This, too, can be labor-intensive, "hard" work.

In our past and present debates over *truth* in the church (both Brethren and other denominations), it is sad to note how often we pursue truth at the expense of love. "Divide and conquer" and "win at all costs" attitudes have no place in the church. The authentic community of faith can lovingly affirm biblical truth and church discipline in times of sin, without adopting the vengeful, spiteful attitudes that are so often seen in the world.[6]

c. Patience inspired by hope. Our hope as Christians is focused on one event: the resurrection from the dead, for the resurrection signifies our salvation. When God raised Jesus from the dead, a decisive, universe-changing event happened. The powers of this world were shown not to have ultimate control over the fate of people. The powers of this age may seek ill of believers. They may even kill believers, but they have no ultimate power. Our patient hope helps us affirm with Jesus, "And do not fear those who kill the body but cannot kill the soul" (Matthew 10:28).

Because of this hope, Christians can live with patience, waiting for the day when salvation will be revealed. Patience is the self-control shown when tempted to choose a way other than God's way. When revenge looks like an attractive possibility, Jesus' teaching is to "turn the other cheek," showing patience that Jesus' ways are the correct ways. Peter's question to Jesus about how many times he should forgive his brother (Matthew 18:21) reflects another opportunity for patience. When tempted to choose another course of action, we see that the way of Jesus is to forgive, patiently hoping that a sister or brother will learn another way.

Paul's thanksgiving for the lives of the Thessalonians includes "knowing...your election by God." The doctrine of election has been one of the more controversial doctrines in Christian history, with different understandings and em-

---

[6]   Concerning the Church of the Brethren heritage and the three-way split of the early 1880s, it is commonly thought that while the split with the conservative branch of the church (today's Old German Baptist Brethren) was probably unavoidable, the split with the progressive branch of the church (today's Brethren Church) might not have happened, had more work been done to achieve both truth *and* love. See Donald Durnbaugh, *Fruit of the Vine*, chapter 14 for more on this topic.

phases made from the pages of Scripture.

While having a full and proper understanding of the doctrine of election is a necessary thing, one must be careful not to over-interpret every reference. Paul does not set forth the entire doctrine of election in these verses. In fact, he says very little about it, other than to state the fact of the Thessalonians election. What Paul affirms in this reference is that God has always desired a group of people set apart for His purposes, whose job it is to proclaim God's goodness. The Thessalonians are in the same tradition as the Hebrew slaves (Exodus 19:5-6), the Corinthian Christians (1 Corinthians 1:26-31), and the dispersed Christians who received Peter's first letter (1 Peter 1:1, 2:9-10). They have been chosen by God for this same special purpose. The following verses show that the Thessalonians proved worthy recipients of the title "elect."

3. Three signs of the authentic gospel (1:5-8)

Having expressed thanksgiving for the lives of the Thessalonians, Paul now shares thanksgiving for how the gospel produced such a life in them.

(1:5-8) For our gospel did not come to you in word only, but also in power, and in the Holy Spirit and in much assurance, as you know what kind of men we were among you for your sake. And you became followers of us and of the Lord, having received the word in much affliction, with joy of the Holy Spirit, so that you became examples to all in Macedonia and Achaia who believe. For from you the word of the Lord has sounded forth, not only in Macedonia and Achaia, but also in every place. Your faith toward God has gone out, so that we do not need to say anything.

Mark Twain is reported to have said, "I'm not concerned about the parts of the Bible I don't understand. What concerns me are the parts I do understand." This is in some measure a healthy attitude, although believers should always seek to grow in their understanding of *all* parts of the Bible.

The gospel is not a popular item in society these days. Many want to reduce the teachings of the Scripture to just one of many holy books, something like a spiritual pot-luck, where people go down the line and choose a little bit of this and a little bit of that, depending on what suits them. Worse than this are those who view the gospel as a useless relic of a bygone time. Nevertheless, for those who take the time to approach the gospel with open-minded humility, they find that the gospel is "the power of God to salvation for everyone who believes" (Romans 1:16). Paul affirms several truths about the authentic gospel that the Thessalonians demonstrate in their living.

a. The gospel comes with both power and the Holy Spirit. It has been said that "you can lead a horse to water, but you can't make it drink." This is a fair description of evangelism. Christians can preach the gospel, review a tract with a person, describe the lives of great saints of the church, but it is not in their human power to save anyone. Paul refers to just this fact in 2 Corinthians 4:4, where he describes non-believers as those "whose minds the god of this age has blinded." It is only as the Holy Spirit convicts people of sin, melting away their hardness of heart, that individuals will respond to Jesus' invitation to "Come, follow me."

Christians, however, should not use this truth as an excuse from the work of evangelism, for the gospel they share comes with power. "Power" comes from the Greek *dunamis*, a word related to our English word "dynamite." Just as an excavator can use a small amount of dynamite to move a large amount of rock, so believers use the power of the gospel for much spiritual gain. The Holy Spirit still relies on Christians to be active in spreading the gospel. We cannot claim as Moses did that we are "slow of speech and slow of tongue" (Exodus 4:10), for the Holy Spirit does not need our eloquence. We should view the work of evangelism with much humility, prayer, and bold assurance that God is already working in the life of the person we would lead to Jesus, and will provide the spiritual "dynamite" needed at the proper time. In our technical, results-oriented age, we must recognize that evangelism first requires much prayer, preparing the way spiritually for our outreach efforts.

b. The gospel comes with much assurance. When people first come to salvation, there is a natural emotional high. The presence of the Lord is close, and there is much excitement and energy in this new-found life.

As with all new things, however, the newness eventually wears off and enthusiasm wanes. Sadly, many persons lose interest in spiritual things at this point. Prayer time and Scripture reading become less regular. Participation in the life of the church seems like a burden instead of a joy-filled activity. This is a critical time in the life of a Christian, because an important change is taking place. Instead of relying on feelings, the assurance of the gospel must take center stage. Feelings will come and go. What must remain steady is the assurance, the certainty of the truth of the gospel, and God's great love for His children. In spite of outward circumstances, Christians can live with assurance in the good news of Jesus Christ. When personal feelings about the gospel take a lesser place and assurance of the gospel takes control of their spiritual life, believers have found a firm foundation upon which to build their faith and life in Christ.

c. The gospel produces changed lives. Paul is thankful for the Thessalonians because the gospel has produced changed lives. In verse 6, Paul notes that "you became followers of us and of the Lord." A more literal translation of "followers" is "imitators" (NIV). Paul will have more to say about being an imitator in chapter 2. For now, he notes that being a follower of the Lord brings with it both sufferings shared with those who believe (verse 6) and a life that is different from the world around it (verse 7). Though Paul says in verse 8 that "we do not need to say anything" about their faith, Paul clearly delights in boasting about the work of God being accomplished in and through them.

As Christians living in the United States, writing about suffering is difficult because American Christians experience so little of it.[7] Even when the government passes laws that are against gospel values, it is a stretch to call this persecution.

Anabaptist history, however, contains many examples of believers holding strongly to their beliefs even at great personal cost.[8] The trials faced by young men imprisoned during times of war for refusing military service tell an inspiring story all Christians should know. One would do well to research similar examples in our local congregations, and lift these up as examples to be followed.

4. Two signs of authentic conversion (1:9-10)

Paul concludes his thanksgiving for the lives of the Thessalonian Christians by briefly describing their conver-

---

[7] Although not written from an Anabaptist/Pietist perspective, David Limbaugh's book *Persecution* outlines current forms of persecution Christians face in the United States. The examples he cites relate to instances where Christians have been denied the right to publicly express their faith, or are exposed to "multiculturalism" and "tolerance" which promotes all faiths as equal and denies the exclusive claims of the gospel.

[8] For a Church of the Brethren treatment on this topic, See Donald Durnbaugh, *Fruit of the Vine,* chapters 3, 8, 13, and 19. N. Geraldine Plunkett's book *Nathan's Secret* relates this same point in a powerful and understandable way. The writings of Menno Simons and *Martyr's Mirror* provide a broader Anabaptist account of this topic.

sion. He speaks of two signs of conversion.[9] Authentic conversion involves both present activity and future hope.

(1:9-10) For they themselves declare concerning us what manner of entry we had to you, and how you turned to God from idols to serve the living and true God, and to wait for His Son from heaven, whom He raised from the dead, even Jesus who delivered us from the wrath to come.

a. Authentic conversion involves turning from idols to serve God. Conversion must produce a noticeable change of life. The most serious obstacle the church puts in front of non-believers is that of Christians who proclaim Jesus with their lips but deny Him with their lifestyle. Authentic conversion will involve a change of attitude and practice from those behaviors the world finds acceptable. These idols include strong drink, sports, workaholism, seeking status or wealth, sexual practices other than singleness or committed heterosexual marriage, or any of a whole host of other idols of this age. Conversion means leaving these things behind and turning to serve God.

The book *Preaching in a Tavern* includes a helpful illustration concerning authentic conversion. "On his return from evangelistic work, Rufus P. Bucher encountered a young stranger in a railway depot who handed him a tract entitled 'Brother, Are You Saved?' When the young man put that same question to Bucher, the Church of the Brethren farmer-preacher replied, 'That is a good question and deserves an answer. I think, however, that I might be prejudiced in my own behalf. You better go down to Quarryville [Pennsylvania] and ask George Hensel, the hardware merchant, what he thinks about it. Or you might go to the Mechanic Grove grocer or to one of my neighbors in Unicorn.

---

[9] *NIV Study Bible,* study note for 1 Thessalonians 1:9-10, page 1821. I have reduced the number of points from three to two.

While there, you might ask my wife and children. I'll be ready to let their answers stand as my own.'"[10]

b. Authentic conversion means waiting for the Son. What a reason we have to be thankful! One day, we will experience the return of Jesus. This is a topic Paul will turn to in greater depth later in the epistle. But for now, we take great assurance that the here and now is not the object of our living. We are moved to worship by the future reality of the reign of God. One day, "God will wipe away every tear from their eyes; there shall be no more death, nor sorrow, nor crying. There shall be no more pain, for the former things have passed away" (Revelation 21:4). For those countless Christians through the ages who knew trouble and persecution, what a great hope this is! Turning from idols to serve God may bring trouble, as it did for many believers of past ages. It also brings great hope for the return of the Son.

---

[10] Kenneth I. Morse, "Are You Saved?"—"Ask My Neighbor," *Preaching in a Tavern*, number 53.

Chapter 2

THE APOSTLES' WORK AMONG THE THESSALONIANS
1 Thessalonians 2:1—3:13

First Thessalonians chapters two through five are the body of the epistle. In these chapters, there are two distinct sections. Chapters two and three describe the apostles' work in Thessalonica and the effect they hoped it would have. Chapters four and five (through 5:22) contain instruction on several points related to the specific concerns of the Thessalonian believers. Chapters two and three are the focus of this section of the commentary. In these two chapters, the letter reads mostly like personal mail and reflects Paul's feelings toward the Thessalonians. Acts 17:1-10 gives the historical background to the events Paul describes in this chapter. Paul, Silvanus, and Timothy encountered great opposition in Thessalonica from some Jews who were "unpersuaded" and "envious" (Acts 17:5). These troublemakers stirred up a violent mob, and the three evangelists were forced to leave town quickly, much earlier than they intended. This early departure from Thessalonica was very troubling to Paul, as he had come to love the Thessalonians quite deeply, and was concerned about their spiritual growth and maturity.

Paul's comments in these two chapters involve two main themes: defending himself from those in the opposition party who are calling his teaching and character into question, and encouraging the Thessalonians because of their trials.

Concerning the opposition, Paul is not simply defending himself for his own benefit. Instead, he is relating a

31

known historical fact (the severe opposition he encountered) to make the greater point that the presentation of the gospel moves persons to a saving faith. These persons then become imitators of Christ and of other Christians, even when faced with persecution. This is exactly what happened in Thessalonica. Paul uses both the conflict he encountered and the deep love he had for the Thessalonians to encourage their new faith.

Paul encourages the Thessalonians in the face of their trials, telling them that the trials are an indication of their faithfulness—a point Paul instructed them about during his visit.

Chapters two and three of 1 Thessalonians are far more personal than they are systematic. Unlike chapters four and five, these chapters do not contain detailed teaching and instruction. Nevertheless, Paul's deep love for the Thessalonians is connected to the faith they profess, and as such, provides many rich examples for living today.

1. The apostles handled the gospel faithfully (2:1-6)

Conflict is never easy to handle. When persons disagree with one another over issues that are deeply held, hurt feelings, anger, and even varying degrees of violence are often experienced. Ironically, when the conflict concerns spiritual issues, the negative feelings are typically stronger. Yet, the reality is that there will always be conflict, at least until the Lord returns.

Often, Christians act as if conflict in the church is a bad thing that should be avoided at any cost. Some congregations avoid conflict by "sweeping things under the rug" to keep from "losing members." Others avoid conflict by aligning themselves only with those who think "like them" in an effort to drive out those with whom they disagree.

As Paul defends himself in the face of the conflict encountered at Thessalonica, his comments give insight into the role of the gospel—and those who preach its message—in those times when there is conflict concerning God's Word.

(2:1-2) For you yourselves know, brethren, that our coming to you was not in vain. But even after we had suffered before and were spitefully treated at Philippi, as you know, we were bold in our God to speak to you the gospel of God in much conflict.

Thessalonica was not the first place where Paul and his ministry team had encountered opposition. Before arriving in Thessalonica they had been in Philippi. Paul and Silvanus had been beaten and imprisoned before being asked to leave the town (Acts 16:12-40). Now that they have also encountered more trouble in Thessalonica, some apparently suggested that their work had not been worth the trouble.

Paul, however, does not measure the value or success of his work by those standards. He says that the work "was not in vain." "In vain" translates the Greek *kenos*, which literally means "empty" or "empty handed," and can be used to suggest uselessness, foolishness, or ineffectiveness. Does the severe opposition mean that Paul's presentation of the gospel and the time invested in the lives of these believers was empty or useless? Quite the contrary. The evangelists were "bold in our God" as they preached the gospel. They were undeterred in the face of opposition because they understood several key things about the nature of the gospel.

Paul was confident in the work because, first, he understood that the presentation of the gospel will cause a certain amount of conflict. Conflict and persecution are nothing new to the lives of believers, as was briefly mentioned in chapter 1 of this commentary. Nevertheless, whether the conflict is as severe as persecution or as mild as strong discussions by those who interpret the Scriptures differently, some measure of conflict should be expected when the true gospel is preached. The gospel challenges sin, and despite its long-term effects, people like their sin. Sadly, many oppose those who bring the message of life because they are comfortable in their sin. Jesus' teaching in John 16:33 provides comfort in such times: "In the world you will have tribulation; but be of good cheer, I have overcome the world."

(2:3) For our exhortation did not come from error or uncleanness, nor was it in deceit.

A second reason the work was not "in vain" was because of the moral purity of those presenting the gospel. It has been suggested that some of Paul's comments here and later in chapter 2 are intended to "differentiate himself from other popular preachers of philosophy and religion of his day."[11] Such persons offered messages that were contrary to the gospel, and many of the evangelists were nothing more than charlatans, seeking a gullible audience that would help line their own pockets.

It is worth noting that Paul could not be accused of some moral failure. Some may have tried to accuse him, but such an approach was doomed to failure because of Paul's moral standard. It seems almost a daily occurrence in our time that a Christian leader is accused of some moral failure which ruins both family and ministry, causes division in the church, and brings great shame to the name of Jesus.[12] But Paul can affirm that the work he shared with Silvanus and

---

[11]   Jacob W. Elias, *1 & 2 Thessalonians, Believers Church Commentary*, page 66.

[12]   See *BRF Witness*, "Dangers that Confront Preachers," Volume 40, Number 2, March-April 2005.

Timothy was conducted with great integrity, and was not "in vain" due to some moral lapse. The opposition may have opposed the message, but they could find no moral fault in the messengers. May God's servants of this generation seek to be found in a similar light.

(2:4-5) But as we have been approved by God to be entrusted with the gospel, even so we speak, not as pleasing men, but God who tests our hearts. For neither at any time did we use flattering words, as you know, nor a cloak for covetousness—God is witness.

A third reason Paul felt comfortable about his work was that he did not go to Thessalonica to please people. One popular summary of the pastor's job is to "comfort the afflicted and afflict the comfortable." Such a task does not make for easy preaching. There is much in the gospel that brings great measure of comfort and hope, as Christians contemplate theirr glorious salvation. But before salvation occurs, there must be repentance. Not many want to hear such a message, but the way to life lies through the door of repentance. Such a message must be preached, "in season and out of season," and not to satisfy "itching ears" (2 Timothy 4:2-3).

(2:6) Nor did we seek glory from men, either from you or from others, when we might have made demands as apostles of Christ.

Finally, Paul is confident in his work because he was not seeking to add to his reputation. Here again Paul sets the ministry of him and the others apart from those who preach out of impure motive. The evangelists sought to be neither "flattering" nor receive "glory from men." As mentioned above, there were many traveling preachers in that day, presenting many spiritual alternatives. These preachers often had a "high maintenance" lifestyle. They expected a great deal of attention, including the expectation of being well paid and cared for while they preached in a particular location. Although Paul, Silvanus, and Timothy could have made similar demands, they did not. Ironically, some people doubted their authenticity because they did not live up to the trendy image. Instead of using the gospel to attract attention to themselves, they simply presented the gospel in word and deed, making disciples along the way. While some chose flashy methods, Paul and his companions sought solid results.

2. The apostles loved the church faithfully (2:7-12)

Continuing the defense against those who questioned his work and integrity, Paul now shifts his focus. Whereas the previous six verses discussed the presentation and nature of the gospel, Paul now describes the attitude he, Silvanus, and Timothy had as they lived and worked among the Thessalonians. The images in these verses are deeply personal and familial.

A first glance at these comments might lead persons to assume they apply only to the lives of pastors. Clearly, churches would do well to have pastors who live their lives in such a manner. These qualities, however, are to be commended to any leader in the church–deacon, moderator, Sunday School teacher, music minister, youth leader, etc. They are the qualities of those who understand that ministry is not about program, but about people.

(2:7) But we were gentle among you, just as a nursing mother cherishes her own children.

Paul and his companions could clearly have made demands on the Thessalonians. Instead, they chose a different method. Rather than acting like the popular, non-Christian traveling preachers of the day, they were *gentle* among the

Thessalonians, not making demands, though they may have been within their rights to do so.

Paul's description of just how they were "gentle among you" is a wonderfully deep metaphor. In the Greek language, Paul compares their efforts to that of a *trophos*. The NKJV translates this word as "nursing mother." Other translations use simply "mother" (NIV); or "nurse" (NRSV). From the known meaning of the word *trophos*, it would appear that Paul intended to suggest both meanings of the word: they were like a nurse, in that they *diligently* cared for the Thessalonians because that was their job as apostles. They were like a mother in that they *lovingly* cared for the Thessalonians because that was the depth of their heart. Michael Holmes describes this dual metaphor by saying "as a nurse fulfills her duty by caring for others and goes beyond duty in cherishing her own [family], so the missionaries fulfill their obligation by sharing the gospel and go beyond obligation by sharing themselves."[13]

Connecting this metaphor to our lives is not difficult at all. Nurses have very difficult jobs as they give of themselves to provide care for people. Often, this care comes in times of crisis—times when people are "not themselves." So it is with mission work. If people are less than what they were created to be until they come to know the Savior, sharing the gospel is also work among people who are "not themselves."

The mothering image is even easier to relate. One only has to think of (or remember!) the look in the eyes of a mother as she holds her baby for the first time to understand the depths of love the apostles had for the Thessalonians.

---

[13]   Michael W. Holmes, *1 & 2 Thessalonians, NIV Application Commentary*, page 65.

This depth of love explains the lengths to which they went to help them experience the fullness of life in Christ.

(2:8-10) So, affectionately longing for you, we were well pleased to impart to you not only the gospel of God, but also our own lives, because you had become dear to us. For you remember, brethren, our labor and toil; for laboring night and day, that we might not be a burden to any of you, we preached to you the gospel of God. You are witnesses, and God also, how devoutly and justly and blamelessly we behaved ourselves among you who believe;

The role of the apostle and pastor is to be involved in the life of the congregation, leading the flock into the depths and riches of a life-changing encounter with Jesus Christ. Paul, Silvanus, and Timothy accomplished this by living among the Thessalonians, working for a living while preaching the gospel.

During the twentieth century, the form of pastoral leadership went through a transition in Mennonite and Brethren churches. The historical model for both traditions has been the "free ministry" (the Brethren term) or the "supported ministry" (the Mennonite term). In the last approximately fifty years, however, pastoral models shifted to paid, seminary-trained, professional clergy. In spite of the shift, "free" or "supported" ministry remains a vital source of congregational leadership. As Brethren and Mennonite churches face the realities of ministry in the twenty-first century, continuing pastoral shortages are requiring a return of the free and supported ministry.[14]

Finding Scripture that lends support to either model is possible. Paul's comments in these verses, however, do lend

---

[14] For further information about pastoral shortages and free ministry in the Church of the Brethren, see the November 2004 *Messenger*. For Mennonites, see: http://www.mennoniteusa.org/executive/ministerial_leadership/docs/call.

support and encouragement for those in bi-vocational ministry. Clearly, this is a vital topic for churches of this day. The lesson in Paul's words is that free ministry models do not burden the resources of the congregation with the requirements of a salary, and encourage all believers to become involved in the work of evangelism.

(2:11) as you know how we exhorted, and comforted, and charged every one of you, as a father does his own children,

Earlier, Paul used the nurturing image of a mother to describe the mission work. Now he shifts to the image of a loving father. In this metaphor, Paul highlights what is often seen in the relationship between a father and child—that of teaching, correcting, and showing. Loving fathers are involved in the lives of their children, showing them the world, encouraging them to grow and stretch into new skills, and correcting them when they stray into wrong behavior. Paul understood that there are times in the life of a believer when these fatherly qualities must be shown.

God has given mothers and fathers different gifts to use together in raising children; as a good pastor, Paul understood and displayed both characteristics among the Thessalonians.

(2:12) that you would walk worthy of God who calls you into His own kingdom and glory.

All of the qualities Paul, Silvanus, and Timothy displayed in their work among the Thessalonians were for a distinct purpose: that the Thessalonians would display a certain kind of life. Paul was not simply filling a position in the church. He was not running a program or doing "maintenance ministry." God sent him to Thessalonica to preach the gospel. The gospel brings certain expectations of life and faith and Paul's ministry efforts were geared to those expectations. He expected that certain qualities would be displayed in those who accepted the message of salvation, and he ministered— with the loving nurture of a mother and with the shaping and exhorting guidance of a father—that the Thessalonians might "walk worthy of God."

3. The apostles created imitators (2:13-16)

As Paul continues encouraging the Thessalonians to "walk worthy of God" in light of Christ's return, he again changes his focus, this time to thank God for the effect the work had in the lives of the Thessalonians. Paul sees evidence that the Thessalonians have truly received the gospel.

In these four verses, there are two main points of interest: first, the notion of being an *imitator*, and second, understanding Paul's rather strong words concerning "the Judeans" and the wrath that has come upon them.

(2:13) For this reason we also thank God without ceasing, because when you received the word of God which you heard from us, you welcomed it not as the word of men, but as it is in truth, the word of God, which also effectively works in you who believe.

Paul starts this section with a spontaneous thanksgiving for the lives of these believers. He begins his comments by giving the reason for the thanks: it is because the Thessalonians received the word of God "as it is in truth." They believed it to be the word of God, and not a good idea created by people.

Many today debate the nature of the Bible and find it difficult to "welcome" it as a source of truth and authority in their lives. Is the gospel merely "good teaching" by a "moral teacher?" Is the Scripture one of any number of possible choices offered on some sort of "spiritual buffet," all of which are equally good, depending on the tastes of the chooser? Perhaps some of the Thessalonian believers first responded to Paul's teaching with such questions. In light of our pluralistic, multi-cultural world, what is the best way to approach the Scripture, especially with someone who is skeptical about its authority?

A starting point is found in these verses. First, take the gospel at face value. Rather than finding fault with the Scripture, deal with what it says and seek to apply it to living. Verse 13 describes the word of God as something which "effectively works in you who believe." Those who seek to take the Scripture at face value have found within the word of God itself the Spirit of God who inspires these words. As Hebrews 4:12 says, "For the word of God is living and powerful, and sharper than any two-edged sword, piercing even to the division of soul and spirit, and of joints and marrow, and is a discerner of the thoughts and intents of the heart." All Christians can testify to times when they have been reading the Scripture, and instead "found the Scripture reading them," in the sense of being convicted of sin, or addressing a current situation in their life.

(2:14) For you, brethren, became imitators of the churches of God which are in Judea in Christ Jesus. For you also suffered the same things from your own countrymen, just as they did from the Judeans,

A second answer to one pondering the claims of the Bible is to point to the changed lives of those who believe. The Thessalonians became *imitators* of the "churches of God that are in Judea in Christ Jesus." It is important to note what this "imitation" involved. In the context of this epistle, becoming an imitator involved more than a change of life-style. Becoming an imitator included suffering persecution in a manner similar to the Judean Christians. It also refers to that suffering experienced by Paul that was described earlier. When considering the claims of the Scripture, one would do well to consider the lives of those countless Christians who responded to Christ's call knowing that suffering and even death would be a result of their "imitating" the churches of Christ.

The idea of "imitating" has been an important understanding of faith in the Anabaptist and Pietist traditions. Early Brethren and Mennonites were quite diligent in their study of the New Testament, especially the book of Acts, to understand better how the first Christians lived. Their interest in "primitive Christianity" also led these persons to study early church histories for further testimony of the lives of the saints. The book *Martyrs Mirror* was one such resource. *Martyrs Mirror* is a gripping account of the lives of Anabaptists in Europe in the 1500s, filled with historical accounts of faithful Christians facing suffering, loss, and death because of their commitment to Jesus Christ. The book is made even more compelling because of the graphic illustrations. The illustrations served as an example to encourage imitating (hopefully in "spirit" more than reality).

Such "imitation" influenced the Anabaptists and Pietists in several important ways. One was the idea of believer's baptism. The first generations of Mennonites and Brethren had been baptized as infants. Studying the Scripture led them to conclude that following Jesus was a choice an adult must make, a choice that must be publicly indicated by baptism. In those times re-baptism was a crime, and many believers were severely punished through banishment from their home territories, removal of children from the home, confiscation of property, and even death.

Imitation also influenced church life. In the Church of the Brethren, this imitation of the early church included careful attention to the form of baptism (by trine immersion), the importance and the order of Love Feast, the role of the

Council meeting, anointing, and the holy kiss. These practices were understood as earthly ways to understand the grace received at their salvation, and were held in high regard by past generations.

In thinking about those faithful Christians who have experienced (and continue to experience) severe persecution, the words of a hymn found in the *Ausbund* (an early Anabaptist hymn book) are helpful. Verse three of the hymn *The Word of God is Solid Ground* describes the attitude of many faithful Christians:

> What God-word brings, may we embrace;
>> success and suff'ring greet us;
> Confronting evil face to face,
>> as scorn and anger meet us.
> For freedom's sake we bend, we break,
>> a sign to ev'ry nation
> that we have found a solid ground;
> God's word our sure foundation.[15]

As an aside to the thoughts here, it is worth mentioning other New Testament occurrences of the word "imitate" and the persons or groups commended for imitation, beyond God's churches:

- Paul (and other apostles): 1 Corinthians 4:16, 11:1; Philippians 3:17, 4:9; 1 Thessalonians 1:6; 2 Thessalonians 3:7.
- The Lord: 1 Thessalonians 1:6
- God: Ephesians 5:1
- Godly leaders: Hebrews 6:12, 13:7
- What is "good," as displayed in persons: 3 John 1:11

(2:14b-16) For you also suffered the same things from your own countrymen, just as they did from the Judeans, who killed both the Lord Jesus and their own prophets, and have

---

[15] *Hymnal: A Worship Book*, # 314.

persecuted us; and they do not please God and are contrary to all men, forbidding us to speak to the Gentiles that they may be saved, so as always to fill up the measure of their sins; but wrath has come upon them to the uttermost.

The second important idea in this section involves Paul's seemingly harsh, almost anti-Semitic comments beginning with the phrase "just as they did from the Judeans" in verse 14, and continuing on through verse 16. What is particularly troubling about these verses is that they may be misinterpreted as a blanket condemnation of all Jews, at least all Jews of Paul's day. Some have used them as an excuse to persecute Jewish persons.

Giving proper attention to the context shows that these verses are not anti-Semitic at all. Instead, Paul is making a comparison of the Thessalonians' experience of persecution to that of the Judean churches. Both groups were opposed and persecuted by a group of Jewish persons who were opposed to the presence of these followers of Christ. Such persons, Paul writes, are filling up "the measure of their sins." His words should not be extended past this comparison. These verses are specific words for a specific situation, not a blanket generalization to be used as an excuse for Christians to return "an eye for an eye" in this or any other age.

Paul's final comment about these Jewish persecutors is interesting. He says that wrath *has come upon them* to the uttermost. What is this wrath? Have these Judeans experienced it at the time of Paul's writing?

To answer these questions, it is helpful to look at Romans 1:18-32. Paul begins those verses by saying "the wrath of God is revealed from heaven against all ungodliness and unrighteousness of men" before going on to describe several instances of that unrighteousness. Several times in the verses that follow, Paul says God "gave them up" to whatever it was the people were pursuing. God's wrath is seen as receiving what some might call their "just desserts," or, the natural consequences of their choices. The consequences of our choices have present earthly and spiritual results as well as future spiritual results.

Simply put, God allows people a choice. Some, like the Thessalonians, will receive the word of truth and become imitators of earlier generations of Christians. Such persons will be the cause of great thanksgiving. Others, sadly, will not follow; others will even become persecutors of Christ and the church. Such persons store up wrath for themselves. When the measure of wrath is full, it will overflow, and people will experience God's judgment in the consequences of their choices. In this sense, the Judeans Paul refers to have received God's wrath. God has allowed them to make choices that led them away from God. If they did not turn from their sin, more wrath will come.

4. The apostles longed to return (2:17—3:10)

Paul's deeply personal comments to the Thessalonians continue, but, as with 2:7 and 2:13, his focus shifts to a different aspect of the love he has for them and their faith in Jesus. The two major topics in this section are Paul's desire to see the Thessalonians in person and some further comments concerning the nature of trials.

(2:17-18) But we, brethren, having been taken away from you for a short time in presence, not in heart, endeavored more eagerly to see your face with great desire. Therefore we wanted to come to you—even I, Paul, time and again—but Satan hindered us.

Paul expresses some deeply emotional and personal feelings in expressing his desire to return to see the Thessalonians. Some (either friend or foe) have likely interpreted his absence as abandonment—he either did not love the Thessalonians or could not handle the pressure.

Whatever the Thessalonians may have been thinking, Paul goes to great lengths to assure them that they have been foremost in his thoughts and prayers. His language is again that of the family; the NJKV phrase "having been taken away" translates the Greek *aporphanizo*, which literally means "to make an orphan of." Normally, one thinks of orphans as children who have lost their parents, but in the Greek the word can be applied to parents who have lost their children.

Furthermore, Paul says that he had "great desire" to see them. He uses the same word in the Greek that describes the desire the beggar Lazarus had to eat the scraps from the rich man's table (Luke 16:21) and the desire Jesus had to eat the Last Supper with the disciples (Luke 22:15). It is a word that expresses desire in the strongest of terms.

For those in Thessalonica who may have been wondering, Paul does give a reason for his absence–Satan hindered him. This is a point that is worth careful attention. Some today over-sensationalize the demonic, seeing, as it were, a "demon behind every bush." Such persons believe "the devil made me do it" explains every sinful action. Others, however, take the opposite approach and see every obstacle in merely human terms as something to be overcome through greater effort, power of persuasion, luck, or other human trait.

Paul's understanding of Satan, however, falls between these extremes. Though Satan was defeated through Christ's resurrection from the grave, Satan is still at work, walking around like "a roaring lion" (1 Peter 5:8). In Paul's case, this "roaring" takes the shape of members of the opposition party, whose hostility prevented Paul's return to Thessalonica to instruct the young church. Thanks be to God that, as a defeated power, we may stand and be victorious over Satan's schemes through the blood of Jesus and the "whole armor of God" (Ephesians 6:11).

(2:19-20) For what is our hope, or joy, or crown of rejoicing? Is it not even you in the presence of our Lord Jesus Christ at his coming? For you are our glory and joy.

Paul here shows why he feels so strongly about the Thessalonians. He desires that they be found faithful, because their faithfulness will serve as a sign of authenticity of their receiving the gospel. Paul wants no crown, no earthly reward for his labors. The only reward he seeks will be found in the life and faith of these persons.

To hear Jesus tell those who were under his leadership "Well done, good and faithful servant" is the highest desire for any Christian leader. This is what it means to "build on this foundation" [the Lord Jesus Christ] "with gold, silver, [and] precious stones." Such work will be found worthy of reward (1 Corinthians 3:12-14).

(3:1-5) Therefore, when we could no longer endure it, we thought it good to be left in Athens alone, and sent Timothy, our brother and minister of God, and our fellow laborer in the gospel of Christ, to establish you and encourage you concerning your faith, that no one should be shaken by these afflictions; for you yourselves know that we are appointed to this. For, in fact, we told you before when we were with you that we would suffer tribulation, just as it happened, and you know. For this reason, when I could no longer endure it, I sent to know your faith, lest by some means the tempter had tempted you, and our labor might be in vain.

Chapter 3 begins with Paul admitting that he reached the point where he could not stand the suspense any longer. Timothy was dispatched to Thessalonica to check on their well-being. Specifically, he was sent to strengthen whatever parts of their faith were damaged through persecution, and to build on the work done before.

As has been stated, Paul's concern was over the trials the Thessalonians were experiencing. In 3:3, Paul sheds light on yet another aspect of trials–namely, that "we are appointed to this." In following Christ, the Thessalonians were leaving behind the socially-accepted customs of the day, as is true in this day. Non-Christian friends and family would have been offended by this change. Furthermore, it was commonly thought that "civic peace, agricultural success, and freedom from natural catastrophe were thought to lie in the hands of the traditional gods."[16] It is in this sense that Christians "are appointed" to trials. In following Jesus, Christians make a choice to make their home in a kingdom that has different values from the culture around them. In choosing one, they must reject the other. Such persecution from family, non-believers, or even old "drinking buddies," is part of the trials faithful Christians will face.

A close parallel that can be made to contemporary society is when American Christians turn their back on "American values" because they conflict with the gospel. For all the freedoms afforded to persons living in the United States, there are parts of this culture that Christians properly reject, facing some sort of "trial" or "persecution" as a result. Michael Holmes lists several possibilities of what this might look like:

- an honest employee is fired for disrupting a company's plans to scam consumers or for blowing the whistle on corruption and fraud;

---

[16] Michael W. Holmes, *1 & 2 Thessalonians, NIV Application Commentary*, page 102.

- a law enforcement officer is ostracized and pushed out of line for a promotion by her fellow officers because she refuses to lie in order to cover up misconduct by another officer;
- high school students experience hostility in taking a stand in an environment where social status and standing is heavily dependent on the extent to which one uses alcohol and/or drugs or is sexually active;
- families who refuse to buy into the consumer mentality of our culture, and thereby implicitly challenge those who do, are rejected by neighbors and friends;
- a teacher who refuses parents who demand that their child be given a grade higher than that earned by the student's work receives harsh criticism;
- a person whose consistent pro-life ethic includes opposition not only to abortion, but to the death penalty as well, finds himself or herself as a disliked "persecuted minority."[17]

Other examples might easily be added: refusal to hang an American flag in the sanctuary of the church; refusing selective service; protesting "popular" wars; choosing conscientious objection; or protesting multinational business practices which exploit lower income workers.

(3:6-10) But now that Timothy has come to us from you, and brought us good news of your faith and love, and that you always have good remembrance of us, greatly desiring to see us, as we also to see you—therefore, brethren, in all our affliction and distress we were comforted concerning you by your faith. For now we live, if you stand fast in the Lord. For what thanks can we render to God for you, for all the joy with which we rejoice for your sake before our God, night and day

---

[17] Michael W. Holmes, *1 & 2 Thessalonians, NIV Application Commentary*, page 108.

praying exceedingly that we may see your face and perfect what is lacking in your faith?

These verses resume the discussion of Timothy's trip. Paul can barely contain his enthusiasm upon hearing the report Timothy brought. Earlier in the commentary, some speculation was given as to what Paul, Silvanus, and Timothy might have discussed the night before Paul began to write; his comments here make one think he sat down and began writing immediately! Timothy's report had affirmed Paul's hopes and calmed his fears. The Thessalonians are weathering the storm and Paul's earlier work has been successful. Furthermore, the Thessalonians are as eager to see Paul as he is eager to see them, and their faith serves to strengthen Paul in his current troubles–the encouraged have become the encourager. Though Paul sees some areas for improvement in their lives ("and perfect what is lacking in your faith") Paul's thanksgiving is great indeed.

In verses 8-10, Paul again shows his pastor's heart. Often, when churches seek qualified leaders, they turn to lists of qualifications found in 1 Timothy 3 and Titus 1. The verses under examination here, however, reveal some different characteristics. These verses reveal the heart, a much more difficult thing to measure, to be sure. Paul's thanksgiving is beyond words; his joy is exuberant, and his desire to see them continue in the walk of faith is ever on his lips in prayer. May God grant us pastors such as these!

5. The apostles prayer for the Thessalonians (3:11-13)

These verses bring this section of Paul's very personal comments to an end. What better way to end this section where Paul has encouraged the Thessalonians (and been encouraged by them) than with prayer? In keeping with the overall tone of this section of the letter, Paul's comments are more than a prayer; they serve to model the kind of behavior he hopes the Thessalonians will reflect in their lives, as well as underscoring Paul's belief in both human activity and divine action.

(3:11) Now may our God and Father Himself, and our Lord Jesus Christ, direct our way to you.

Paul had been quite concerned by his inability to return to Thessalonica; now he prays that God will make that trip possible. In checking the book of Acts, one sees that this prayer was answered, as Paul made a return trip to Thessalonica as part of his third missionary journey (see Acts 20:1). Paul's desire to return to Thessalonica demonstrates a healthy understanding of the relationship of divine activity and human effort. His earlier comments make it clear that making this trip was simply not possible for him. God's intervention was required. But Paul's actions in Acts 20 make it clear that more was required than God acting. Paul actually had to make the trip. Such should be our practice–praying for God to do his part, and then we being faithful in doing our part.

(3:12-13) And may the Lord make you increase and abound in love to one another and to all, just as we do to you, so that He may establish your hearts blameless in holiness before our God and Father at the coming of our Lord Jesus Christ with all His saints.

Paul models the same divine action/human activity pattern he did in verse 11 in these verses as well. His prayer is for their spiritual growth; he will give them specific instruction on these points in chapters 4 and 5. He wants the things of God to be reflected in their relationships with one another.

Before that instruction, however, Paul says that this spiritual growth has a long-range purpose. It is that the

Thessalonian believers might be found a certain way when Jesus does return, namely, "blameless in holiness." To be found blameless is only possible through the substitutionary atonement, Jesus Christ taking our place and receiving the punishment for our sin. An immediate benefit to the saving work of Jesus is that when individuals are saved, they are at that moment blameless in God's sight. This is our *justification*. But as individuals walk with God, they are made holy as they grow in their salvation, becoming more mature. This is our *sanctification*. The result of both justification and sanctification is that when Christ returns, we will be "blameless in holiness."

Those outside the church often criticize the church for being filled with "hypocrites." One reason it appears this way is that Christians are still maturing in their faith, moving toward being "blameless in holiness." It reflects the truth about the Christian life that each believer will go through that process of maturing. Encouraging this process of maturing is one purpose of Paul's prayer.

Chapter 3

INSTRUCTIONS FOR GODLY LIVING
1 Thessalonians 4:1-12

Having concluded a lengthy section of personal comments about his love for the Thessalonians, Paul turns his attention in this chapter to providing instruction. In the comments on 1 Thessalonians 1:1, there was speculation on what Paul, Silvanus, and Timothy might have discussed on the night before Paul set out to write. The material found in 4:1—5:22 would have been a major part of that discussion.

It is reasonable to assume that Timothy's visit to Thessalonica and subsequent report influenced Paul's choice of topics in chapters four and five. Timothy spent time with these young, enthusiastic Christians, checking on their spiritual welfare. While there, he discovered some matters of the faith about which the Thessalonians needed further teaching. Timothy brought a list of topics back to Paul; it is these topics to which Paul now turns his attention.

First Thessalonians 4:1-12 has practical instruction on how a Christian can live to please God. Teaching on sexual purity receives the most attention in these verses, and will receive significant discussion here. There are also instructions on brotherly love and responsible living.

One might think that in a passage as seemingly straightforward as this one, the church would be of one mind on its interpretation. Unfortunately that is not the case. One challenge that churches encounter in providing instruction on faithful living, is nurturing *obedience to the Scripture* while avoiding *legalism*. As long as discussions of ethical matters focus on general principles (such as "love your neighbor" or "attend church regularly") then there will be few difficulties. Almost everyone would agree that the church stands for any number of general principles, and that believers ought to support these principles.

It is when the church begins to give instruction about how committed Christians might *helpfully live out* these principles that some will begin to disagree. What one person sees as a logical principle of faithful living, another sees as legalism. Strong debate and difference of opinion are virtually guaranteed, especially when discussing sexual conduct. In striving for obedience, the church must recognize that today's culture is strongly individualistic. People do not like being told what to do, even if it is for their good. This attitude may be *as prevalent in the church* as it is in the society at large. Yet, the church cannot neglect its responsibility to be a "peculiar people" in the world. The church must provide strong teaching and bold witness to the ways of God. In light of current controversies, how is the church to proceed?

1. Introduction (4:1-2)

Paul's approach to this challenge is as helpful to modern readers as it was to the Thessalonians. Rather than beginning with particulars, Paul begins with the notion that we can please God. This is found in 1 Thessalonians 4:1-2.

(4:1-2) Finally then, brethren, we urge and exhort in the Lord Jesus that you should abound more and more, just as you received from us how you ought to walk and to please God; for you know what commandments we gave you through the Lord Jesus.

It would be easy to read over these two verses as merely an introduction or transition to the topic of sexuality, but such an approach would miss a truth that is vital to our growth as Christians. The instructions that follow in this section are not simply a set of rules to be voted up or down.

Instead, they come from the depths of Paul's living relationship with the Lord Jesus Christ, a relationship that motivated Paul to please God. These are not rules for the sake of having rules; they are specific guidelines that will move Christians into a deeper and more faithful walk with the Lord. They do this in two important ways:

a. They encourage Christians to abound. Often, Christians have certain understandings of what authentic Christian behavior looks like. Peter asked, "Lord, how often shall my brother sin against me, and I forgive him? Up to seven times?" (Matthew 18:21). In the same way, people are willing to walk faithfully, to a point. Or many believe that they are capable of certain levels of obedience and service to God, but will never be as faithful as some well-loved saint. In our living, it is easy to forget that God "is able to do exceedingly abundantly above all that we ask or think, according to the power that works in us" (Ephesians 3:20).

It is at this point where Paul's encouragement to abound applies. The word translated "abound" means exceeding what is expected or surpassing the set bounds.[18] Whatever understanding of faithful living Christians may have or others may expect, it can be exceeded because of the power of God at work in all believers.

Such "abounding" shows up in a variety of surprising ways. For example, God has called many men to preach who felt either incapable or afraid. Yet, these persons "abounded" to become some of the best ministers. Some felt unable to share the gospel with another person, and yet "abounded" to find a way of witnessing that is a unique and effective reflection of their gifts and abilities. Some believers have been

---

[18]   T. Brandt, "Fullness, Abound, Multitude, Fulfill, Make Room," *New International Dictionary of New Testament Theology, volume 1*, pages 728-731.

deeply hurt by a friend, but have "abounded" to forgive and find that damaged and broken relationships can be restored.[19]

It is at this point where specific teaching (like that to follow in 4:3-12) applies. Some will not like being "told what to do." Nevertheless, if persons cut themselves off from all forms of disciplined living, they cut themselves off from the means by which they can abound. A benefit of discipline is the strength it gives believers to grow in their relationship with God.

In their book *Caring Like Jesus: The Matthew 18 Project*, Daniel Ulrich and Janice Fairchild offer some very helpful comments on self-discipline that are relevant to the present discussion:

> Self-discipline may seem like a dreary subject consisting of a series of internalized rules and demands; nevertheless, the purpose of self-discipline is not to take away our joy in living. Most of the negative rules in Scripture are like fences designed to keep us from falling into a pit. The pit is what would take away our freedom. The purpose of the fence is to help us stay free so that we can enjoy life as God intended from the beginning.[20]

Guidelines that instruct our living are not intended to be limiting or confining. Instead, they are designed to help us abound, to "exceed what is expected or surpass the set bounds."

---

[19]   One would do well to research stories of both voluntary service workers (Brethren Volunteer Service or Mennonite Voluntary Service, both current and historical) as well as persons involved in new church planting for some insightful illustrations of this point.

[20]   Daniel Ulrich and Janice Fairchild, *Caring like Jesus: The Matthew 18 Project,* page 75.

b. They urge and instruct believers to please God. The word "abounding" describes our relationship with God primarily by the effect it has on individuals. "Pleasing God" shifts the focus of the relationship to the effect such behavior has on God.

It may come as a surprise to some people that they *can* please God—that God might be delighted in their behavior. Christians often have the idea that God is a cold, distant, immovable judge, not unlike the impression one gets in viewing the statue of Abraham Lincoln at the Lincoln Memorial. With such a view of God, the best opinion people might have of their own behavior is that God is standing ready to strike them dead at the first transgression.

Thanks be to God that this picture can be set aside. As Jesus is "the image of the invisible God" (Colossians 1:15), we can look to Jesus to see how it is that God might be pleased by the behavior of His children. Throughout His earthly ministry, Jesus delighted in seeing people experience the life God desires for His children. Jesus' earthly ministry included blessing children, praising faithfulness, and rejoicing with the sick who had been healed. Our view of God is too restrictive if we do not appreciate God for watching and waiting for the prodigal sons and daughters of this world to come home.

An illustration many will understand is that of pleasing earthly fathers. Many persons have pleasant memories as a young child of doing something because we wanted dad to be happy. We swelled up with pride when dad saw our efforts and praised us for them. But though the actions pleased dad, they did not change the "ground rules" of the relationship. We still had to obey. Faithfulness in one action did not mean credit for disobedience later. Yet, our efforts strengthened the relationship as new bonds of closeness were forged through our actions. Pleasing dad is possible. How much more this is true with our heavenly Father. "If you then, being evil, know how to give good gifts to your children, how much more will your Father who is in heaven give good things to those who ask Him!" (Matthew 7:11).

Here again the specific guidelines for Christian living are not intended to be confining. Instead, they are grounded in the belief that persons can have a living, active, joy-filled relationship with God. Keeping this idea at the forefront of our thinking will help us see the need for the specific instructions to which Paul now turns his attention.

2. Instruction one: sexual purity (4:3-8)

The world and the church need a strong, clearly articulated sexual ethic. People today are bombarded with sexual images because advertisers know that sex sells. Furthermore, society has generally adopted an attitude of sexual permissiveness and freedom. Surveys consistently show that a majority of high-school seniors have engaged in sexual intercourse. Provocative dress is the fashion of the day, so much so that little is left to the imagination.

The consequences of this attitude are staggering. AIDS and other sexually transmitted diseases continue to be prevalent. Many in society are interested in human rights and the equality of all persons, but they still evaluate people by how they look. Divorce is epidemic, both inside and outside the church. Very few people address the psychological effect of sexual images occupying so much space in thoughts and attitudes.

The topic of sexuality will always be a difficult one because sexual desire is so much a part of being human. In a world with the attitudes and problems described above, sexual purity is not a popular topic. Sadly, because sexuality has become such a politicized topic in the world and in the church, it has become nearly impossible for the church to speak with clarity (not to mention unity) on this topic. One indicator of just how difficult the topic of sexuality has been for the church is the number of evangelical churches who take strong stands opposing homosexuality and yet have about the same divorce rate in their congregations as does the world. The church in the United States does not speak or live clearly on this issue.

In these verses, Paul outlines four points by which one may live faithfully before God in the area of sexuality.

(4:3) For this is the will of God, your sanctification: that you should abstain from sexual immorality;

a. Sexual purity does please God. The path to sexual purity is first grounded in a desire to please God. The first clause in verse 3 provides a bridge between what Paul just said about pleasing God and how it is that people may begin to do that. It is not enough to want to please God in some abstract sense. There are some particular ways this can be done. For those who are looking for ways to abound in faith and to please God, it can be done.

To say that the instructions given here are "God's will" is to say that God wishes to see these carried out in the lives of His followers. In this day and age it is common to treat statements about "God's will" as debatable points. Such teaching is too often seen as either out of date or intolerant. People who hold such views miss the fact that what God desires in Christian living, is both universal (relevant in all times and places), and beneficial (an aid to our living).

Furthermore, this teaching is believers' "sanctification." Sanctification is not a word used often. In the New Testament, sanctification refers to the process by which God shapes persons into faithful believers. The word comes from the Greek word meaning "make holy" or "set apart," and refers to the idea found throughout the Scripture that God's people are different from the world because they are God's.

For those who follow Christ, seeking to abound and to follow God's will—God will strip away the old desires and attitudes of the world, and in their place provide new desires and attitudes that are in keeping with His will. Such a process can be seen in the attitude of alcoholics, drug addicts, adulterers, criminals, and other sinners who have found a new way of living in Christ.

One of the most helpful illustrations of this point in the Scripture, is Paul's comment in 1 Corinthians 6:9-11. After reciting a list of sinful behaviors, Paul says of the Corinthians, "and such *were* some of you" (emphasis added). They used to be one thing. Now they are something different—a product of sanctification!

Sanctification is the removing of the old, worldly ways and the giving of the new, godly ways. The words of the hymn *Spirit of the Living God* reflect the attitude of the heart that seeks to please God:

> Spirit of the living God, fall afresh on me.
> Spirit of the living God, fall afresh on me.
> Melt me, mold me, fill me, use me.
> Spirit of the living God, fall afresh on me.[21]

b. Abstain from sexual immorality. Once Christians have promised to please God in the area of their sexuality, understanding the boundaries of appropriate sexual behavior is possible. To "abstain from sexual immorality" is to understand God's intentions for humans sexually. Sexual behavior is to be kept within the bounds of the marriage relationship. Any sexual expression outside the husband-wife

---

[21] *Hymnal: A Worship Book*, # 349.

relationship falls into the category of immorality. [22]

(4:4) that each of you should know how to possess his own vessel in sanctification and honor,

c. Possess his own vessel. A third aspect of sexual purity is found in Paul's instruction to "possess his own vessel in sanctification and honor" (verse 4). The essence of this point is the need to maintain self-control. While the prevalence of sexual expression in our society makes the practice of self-control challenging, there are concrete ways to grow stronger in self-control. Christians should identify their own points of weakness and avoid those temptations. This may mean avoiding the magazine rack at the bookstore, and also television programs and movies that are sexually suggestive. In a dating relationship, avoid being alone together, especially late in the evening. It may mean not using the Internet alone. For those times when one is "surprised," either with a sexually suggestive image or a sexually attractive person, avoid long glances and lustful thoughts.

A second aspect of "possessing his own vessel" is also necessary to consider. This involves conducting ourselves so as not to be a stumbling block to other persons. Often we are unaware of the effect our dress has on other persons. This is

---

[22] The current Church of the Brethren statement is found in the 1983 Annual Conference statement, *Human Sexuality from a Christian Perspective.* See (www.brethren.org/ac/ac_statements/83HumanSexuality.htm.) According to the paper, "the church holds to the teaching that sexual intercourse, which can be the most intimate expression of sexuality and the bonding of human relationships, belongs within heterosexual marriage." The current Mennonite Church USA statement is found in the 1987 paper, *A Call to Affirmation, Confession and Covenant Regarding Human Sexuality.* According to this statement, "we understand the Bible to teach that genital intercourse is reserved for a man and a woman united in a marriage covenant...It is our understanding that this teaching also precludes premarital, extramarital and homosexual genital activity.

not to say that we should not take concern for our appearance, but rather to say that some of today's fashionable clothes are sexually suggestive to other persons. We would do well to examine what we wear and consider what effect—intentional or unintentional—it has on other persons.

(4:5-8) not in passion of lust, like the Gentiles who do not know God; that no one should take advantage of and defraud his brother in this matter, because the Lord is the avenger of all such, as we also forewarned you and testified. For God did not call us to uncleanness, but in holiness. Therefore he who rejects this does not reject man, but God, who has also given us His Holy Spirit.

d. Avoid passionate lust. Finally, sexual purity will be achieved as persons "avoid passionate lust." Simply put, Christians need to understand where a lack of self-control will lead on this matter. One needs only to observe society to understand this point. These days, almost any form of sexual behavior between consenting persons is considered acceptable. This is not to be true in the church, and those seeking sexual purity will seek to avoid behaving in a lustful manner.

Paul concludes his instructions on sexual purity in verses 6-8 by returning to where he started: such instruction is grounded in a relationship with God. In verses 1-2, Paul expressed the possibility of a relationship with God in the positive terms of abounding and pleasing God. Here, however, the relationship is expressed in the negative terms of God avenging sin against others, and their rejection of God.

God has made the possibility of a relationship with Him available to all persons. For those who pursue this relationship, Paul's instructions are the means to a fulfilling life in Christ. For those who choose to ignore the relationship by taking advantage and defrauding "his brother," by ignoring God's intentions in the area of sexuality, judgment awaits.

3. Instruction two: brotherly love (4:9-10)

Twice in 1 Thessalonians (here and in 5:1) Paul indicates a subject about which "you have no need that I should write to you." Paul's use of the phrase is a figure of speech that shows the Thessalonians are on the right track concerning the subject, and are encouraged to continue in the way they have been going. His use of the phrase, however, should not be understood to mean that there is nothing to be said; in both instances Paul does provide instruction.

If the reader of this commentary is from an Anabaptist perspective, it is equally true that "you have no need that I should write to you." Mennonite and Brethren history is filled with examples of brotherly love. This love was shown both to individuals within the church community, and to those outside the church. But, like Paul, examples of such love will be given in the commentary below.

(4:9-10) But concerning brotherly love you have no need that I should write to you, for you yourselves are taught by God to love one another; and indeed you do so toward all the brethren who are in all Macedonia. But we urge you, brethren, that you increase more and more;

Verse nine illustrates one positive effect being a follower of Jesus Christ had on the Christians in Thessalonica: they were "taught by God to love one another." The kind of teaching Paul is referring to here is only partly accomplished through sermons, lessons, and other similar teaching endeavors. Teaching truths from the Word of God is an essential ministry of the church that will go a long way in transforming persons from "children of wrath" into persons "alive together with Christ" (Ephesians 2:3-5).

Being "taught by God" is a work the Holy Spirit accomplishes over time as believers spend time in worship, study, fellowship, prayer, and outreach. The deadening effects of sin are literally melted away from hearts as the Spirit transforms persons. Countless Christians can relate stories of old hurts forgiven, old hatreds overcome, selfish attitudes transformed into self-less giving. This is the work of God's Spirit teaching them to love one another. From Paul's comments here, such transformation was clearly happening in the lives of the Christians at Thessalonica, and the love they felt for one another was moving beyond their own congregation into "all Macedonia."

Such brotherly love is also found in great abundance in the more common, everyday examples from living. The practice of "barn-raising" is one example, where church members would gather at a neighbor's farm to build a new barn. In such instances the men would handle the construction, the women would handle the cooking, and the children would help as they were able. Though not many readers have barns anymore, Mennonites and Brethren still come together to raise funds for disaster relief, travel to places where there have been disasters to rebuild homes and take care of children. The bonds of love are greatly strengthened as hammers are swung, nails are driven, and meals are cooked and shared together.

Paul concludes this brief section by urging the Thessalonians to "increase more and more." This instruction is identical to that found in 4:1 where he "urges and exhorts" them to "abound more and more." Paul's wish is that their love for one another would exceed all that anyone might imagine is humanly possible.

4. Instruction three: responsible living (4:11-12)

In concluding this section of "instructions for godly living," Paul again touches on a topic that is found in abundance in Anabaptist and Pietist groups: Christian life should

should be characterized by diligent work.

This topic of physical work is one that is found both here and in 2 Thessalonians 3. The fact that this seemingly minor theme occurs in both letters leads one to wonder if some of the Thessalonians were not working, either out of laziness, or some thought that the Lord's return was imminent. It is entirely possible that Paul is attempting to correct what he sees as a mildly troubling issue in the church.

(4:11-12) that you also aspire to lead a quiet life, to mind your own business, and to work with your own hands, as we commanded you, that you may walk properly toward those who are outside, and that you may lack nothing.

The advice to "lead a quiet life" was one that the Thessalonians needed to heed well because of the persecution they were experiencing. They were simply not able to make much noise or to protest examples of injustice directed toward them. For the Thessalonians, and for many persecuted Christians around the world today, living a quiet life is essential to merely living.

A second aspect of responsible living is that persons earn a living. There are times when life circumstance will require dependance on others for assistance. Such times, however, should be the exception, not the rule. It may be said that Christians should always be willing to help a brother or sister in need but should attempt to live so they are not personally in need. Such attitudes will greatly help persons to "lack nothing."

A final aspect of responsible living may seem to be a contradictory one. Christians will naturally be opposed to much of what the world deems acceptable, even normal. Because they are to live as "His own special people" (1 Peter 2:9), Christians will need to take unpopular stands against the world. Such stands have often led to suffering and death.

Christians are to "walk properly toward those who are outside." Believers may disagree with the world, but are not to be offensive toward the world. One such application of "walking responsibly toward those who are outside" is found in those times when the brotherly love believers had for one another spilled outside the boundaries of the church and was directed towards others, no matter their feelings toward Christ. Christian history is filled with examples of Christians showing great love for one another. In the early years of Christianity, when it was still a persecuted movement, such love often gave believers credibility when they might otherwise have been hated. Christians also often showed great love for all persons, and were known as those who would care for the sick, even at risk of their own lives.

Mennonite scholar Alan Kreider gives an example. He describes early Christians: "Among their activities often were means of serving the material needs of their neighbours which dumbfounded the imagination of their contemporaries. For example, the Christians in Alexandria [Egypt] intervened, on both sides, in a civil war to attempt to mediate a dispute and to bring relief to both parties; the Christians in Carthage [north Africa] nursed the pagan victims of the terrible plague of 252. In many places the Christians provided hospitality and poor relief to pagans as well as believers."[23]

A commitment to godly living will cause Christians to live differently from the world. As they seek to live differently in the area of sexuality, brotherly love, and responsible living, they will find that pleasing God is possible, and will enjoy the close relationship with God that follows as a result.

---

[23] Alan Kreider, *The Change of Conversion and the Origin of Christendom*, page 20.

Chapter 4

INSTRUCTIONS RELATED TO THE
RETURN OF CHRIST
1 Thessalonians 4:13—5:11

The theme of 1 Thessalonians is *faithful living in light of Christ's return*. In each chapter of the epistle Paul briefly mentions the return of Christ; in this section he treats the topic at length. The instruction on the return of Christ is the longest single unit of teaching in the epistle. Clearly, this was a major point of concern in the Thessalonian church, and one on which Paul wished to provide clear instruction. The situation in Thessalonica that generates this teaching is the concern among believers concerning the fate of those of their fellowship who had died. Would they miss the return of Christ? What hope is there for those who die before Christ's return? Paul wished to provide answers to their concerns, and to encourage godly behavior while those who are living wait for Christ to return. As in other parts of the letter, Paul will eventually turn the discussion from Christ's return to matters of daily living.

People today, both inside and outside the church, have a great interest in the end times. The two wars against Iraq have caused many to wonder how Saddam Hussein fits into God's plans for the end of time as we know it. The *Left Behind* series of books have provided one perspective of the end through the lives of fictional characters. Conferences on the topic of biblical prophecy abound. The material provided in 1 Thessalonians 4:13–5:11 is an integral part of understanding the "end times."

One challenge modern readers face in studying these verses is that Paul's teaching in this section often raises more questions than it answers (or even suggests). A careful study of this passage will necessarily be limited to what Paul says here, and will leave other questions for other passages of the Scripture. In these verses, Paul directly addresses the return of Christ, the rapture of Christians, and how to live until these events happen. The commentary that follows will be limited to these topics.

1. Concerning those who have died (4:13-18)

The Thessalonians were concerned about the destiny of those believers who had died before the return of Christ. Paul's teaching provides "hope" and "comfort" to the church by describing the fate of all persons when Jesus does return.

(4:13-14) But I do not want you to be ignorant, brethren, concerning those who have fallen asleep, lest you sorrow as others who have no hope. For if we believe that Jesus died and rose again, even so God will bring with Him those who sleep in Jesus.

The church at Thessalonica was made up of persons whose spiritual backgrounds fit into one of two categories. There were those who had been Jews before their conversion to Christ, and there were those who had been adherents of one of a variety of other religions of the day. Those who had been Jews would have had some understanding of life after death, but for the others, the religions of the day offered little in the way of hope. Most persons raised in Greek culture viewed death as the ultimate end to life. Death was a terrible thing to face, precisely because it was the end, with nothing more to follow.

Because the Christians in Thessalonica were experiencing persecution, it may be that the ones "who have fallen asleep" were martyrs, although this must remain an assumption. Whatever the cause, the death of some of the saints in Thessalonica, combined with a general lack of understanding of everlasting life among the church members, left the congregation feeling hopeless and upset.

Paul's teaching is intended to provide a solid understanding of events when Jesus returns. The teaching will give these Christians a strong reason to hope that their belief in Christ will carry them safely through death. In Christ, there is hope, because the fate of Christians after physical death is tied to the work of Christ Himself. Because Christ rose from the dead, the Christians' destiny when Christ returns has already been determined. What this involves is described in the following verses.

The words, "lest you sorrow as others who have no hope" (verse 13), are not meant to keep God's people from sorrowing or weeping. There is, however, a selfish and unrestrained weeping that is inappropriate for genuine disciples of Jesus.

(4:15-16) For this we say to you by the word of the Lord, that we who are alive and remain until the coming of the Lord will by no means precede those who are asleep. For the Lord Himself will descend from heaven with a shout, with the voice of an archangel, and with the trumpet of God. And the dead in Christ will rise first.

The Thessalonians felt that those who had died before Christ's return were at some tragic disadvantage. Paul's teaching in these verses, however, turns the tables, saying that those who have died actually have an advantage over those who are still alive! What happens on the day of the Lord's return will be experienced first by those who have died. They will be the first to meet the Lord.

One comment needs to be made here about the King James Version translation of verse 15. Where the NKJV reads "will by no means *precede* those who are asleep," the

KJV reads "shall not *prevent* them that are asleep." This is one example of the old language of the King James Version being a hindrance to understanding. The original definition of "prevent" was "to precede," which is the meaning of the Greek word *phothano* used by Paul. Over time, the meaning of the word "prevent" has changed and now means "stop" or "hinder." Paul's point is that faithful followers of Christ will be translated into the presence of the Lord *only after* the dead in Christ shall rise to meet Him.

The events of the Lord's return will be dramatic and will be noticed by all. Just as the arrival of the President of the United States, is often announced by the Marine Corps Band playing *Hail to the Chief*, so it is that the Lord Jesus will shout, alerting the entire world that He is coming. Accompanying the shout of the Lord will be the voice of the archangel and the trumpet of God. Such will make for a glorious moment.

After the fanfare surrounding the announcement of the Lord's return, that which will eventually be experienced by all Christians will be first experienced by those who have died; they will rise to meet the Lord.

The believers' concern had dealt with death; the truth about the Lord's return provided the hope for life.

(4:17) Then we who are alive and remain shall be caught up together with them in the clouds to meet the Lord in the air. And thus we shall always be with the Lord.

Of all that the Bible teaches about people and the spiritual life, one of the more controversial—even outright rejected—topics, is that of the rapture. Many people only consider something believable if they can see it with their eyes, or if it can be "scientifically proven." The idea of Christians suddenly "disappearing" from the face of the earth is often seen as a fairytale. People wonder (and some even joke) about cars without drivers, businesses without employees, and the like.

Nevertheless, to discount the idea of the rapture is to ignore what is plainly written in these verses. The word "rapture" has its roots in verse 17, where Paul says believers will be "caught up" to be with the Lord. "Caught up" translates the Greek *harpazo*, which means "to seize or snatch." The Latin translation is *rapere*, from which comes the English word *rapture*.[24] It is perfectly natural to wonder what this event might be like—whether one begins the journey from death or from life. It is normal to imagine this simply in terms of physically rising with countless other saints to meet Jesus. One might suspect, however, that the experience will be even more than our earthly minds can imagine.

However much persons want to discount the idea of the rapture, the idea of a sudden demonstration of God's power to fully institute the kingdom of God is an idea that is found consistently throughout the Scriptures, in both Old and New Testaments. The "day of the Lord" is a reality that Paul will address directly in chapter 5, and detailed discussion will be reserved until that point. These verses show that the second coming of Christ will be a decisive, clearly established event which Christians will experience first hand. There will be a generation of believers who will not need to go through the valley of the shadow of death.

(4:18) Therefore comfort one another with these words.

What may be the most important truth to take from these verses is that Paul was not writing about Christ's return to provide material for theological outline or debate. Paul did not write as a theologian so much as he did as a pastor.

---

[24]   Michael W. Holmes, *1 & 2 Thessalonians, NIV Application Commentary*, page 151.

Some members of the Thessalonian congregation were experiencing great grief because of their misunderstanding about the nature of death, and even the nature of life. These verses are intended for "comfort" (verse 18) because they show that, alive or dead, Christians are never in a place where God cannot reach them. Death is not an insurmountable barrier in the relationship of the Christian to God. It is merely a phase, a period of time that exists between living for a time here, and living eternally with God. The instruction of verse 18, "comfort one another with these words" should be taken to heart in the church today as much as any instruction of the Scripture.

2. Concerning those who are alive (5:1-11)

Christians of every age and culture have been interested in knowing when Jesus will return. Throughout Christian history, there have been those who speculated when Christ would return. Certain industrious individuals have gone farther, however, and made bold predictions as to the date of Christ's return. This was particularly true around the years 1,000 and 2,000, but it has been true in other eras as well. The abundance of this speculation is interesting, especially considering the fact that the Bible itself provides no information as to the date of Christ's return. Certain signs and indicators are given in various parts of the Bible, but no specific time and date is offered.

The Brethren and Mennonites have not been immune from such end-time speculations. When considering the return of Christ, human nature causes one to ask, "When?" Paul's words in this section answer by saying, "Wrong question!" First Thessalonians 5:1-11 reminds Christians that what is most important is not *when* Jesus will return, but what Jesus will find them doing when He does come.

(5:1-3) But concerning the times and the seasons, brethren, you have no need that I should write to you. For you yourselves know perfectly that the day of the Lord so comes as a thief in the night. For when they say, "Peace and safety!" then sudden destruction comes upon them, as labor pains upon a pregnant woman. And they shall not escape.

Verse one is the second occurrence in the letter of the phrase "no need that I should write to you" (see also 4:9). As before, this is a figure of speech that indicates the Thessalonians already had good understanding on this point. Further instruction serves to encourage their current belief and practice. It is reasonable to assume that Paul spent time instructing the Thessalonians on the return of Christ when he was with them and that they understood his teaching. There was, however, benefit to be gained by providing some additional instruction on this point.

Several points about Christ's return are affirmed in these verses. The "day of the Lord" is a broad term that describes the day Jesus returns to take believers to Heaven and to judge the unrighteous. The phrase "day of the Lord" occurs often in both Testaments. The Old Testament prophet, Zephaniah, talks at length about the day of the Lord, using words like "bitter," "wrath," and "distress" (Zephaniah 1:14-15) to describe the day. Judgment will be levied against those nations who are opposed to God, as well as those who claim to follow the ways of God, but in reality do not. Paul's usage of the phrase "day of the Lord" places the return of Christ in the same tradition as that found in the Old Testament. The return of Christ will mark the ultimate coming of the kingdom of God.

When the end does come, it will come unpredictably, "as a thief in the night," no matter how well persons interpret the signs. Almost everyone takes some precaution to ensure personal safety and security. In this fallen world, thieves do sometimes break in, and taking certain measures to reduce such risks is reasonable. Persons generally do not, however, have guards at their homes every hour of every day to prevent any possible break-in. It is possible that in spite of one's best intentions, thieves will break in and steal.

Similarly, the end will come suddenly, "as labor pains upon a pregnant woman." Today's medical technology makes it possible to predict with some accuracy when a baby will be born, but the moment itself cannot be nailed down with absolute certainty. When the labor pains come, the pregnant mother cannot escape and is caught up in the process of giving birth.

The unpredictability and suddenness of Christ's return is a significant motivating factor for evangelism. Many persons live with the idea that they will put off following Jesus until later. Truly, the gospels teach that those who accept Christ on their deathbed will be as freely received into heaven as those who served Christ many years. What people must understand, however, is that no one is guaranteed to know when his "last moment" will come. It may come through the suddenness of death, or it may come with the unpredictability of Christ's return. Of all of the promises found in the Scripture, "tomorrow" is not guaranteed: "Now is the day of salvation" (2 Corinthians 6:2).

Some will not want to hear this. They will look around at the world and say "all is well." Many in Paul's day seemed to feel this way as well. The phrase "peace and safety" was likely a slogan used by the Roman government[25] to promote the benefits of the empire. Compared with the parts of the

---

[25]   Jacob W. Elias, *1 & 2 Thessalonians, Believers Church Bible Commentary*, page 194.

world that were not under the military and governmental authority of Rome, cities like Thessalonica likely felt peaceful and safe. The Roman government did bring a desirable quality of life to those in the empire.

The coming return of Christ serves as a reminder that there are realities at work in the world beyond what can be seen. The promises of "peace and safety" will be shown to be powerless on the day Christ comes, and no one will avoid this truth. This was true in Paul's day, and it continues to be true today. People who live in the peace and safety of the United States in the twenty-first century must be shown that earthly promises of "peace and safety" will give way to that which is to come from God. A Christian's hope does not ride on what he can see with his eyes. Christians always live with one eye to the heavens, waiting for the return of Christ.

(5:4-8) But you, brethren, are not in darkness, so that this Day should overtake you as a thief. You are all sons of light and sons of the day. We are not of the night nor of darkness. Therefore let us not sleep, as others do, but let us watch and be sober. For those who sleep, sleep at night, and those who get drunk are drunk at night. But let us who are of the day be sober, putting on the breastplate of faith and love, and as a helmet the hope of salvation.

Having stated the point that the return of Christ will be both unpredictable and sudden, Paul turns his attention to how Christians should live in light of Christ's return. Five images are used to describe the quality of being prepared. The first four images contrast the lives of believers from unbelievers: light and dark, day and night, awake and asleep; sober and drunk. The fifth image is a military one, involving preparing for battle.

In presenting the four contrasting images in verses four through seven, Paul provides no particular instruction on how these qualities are to be evident in their lives. Each of the Christian qualities is given as a metaphor. Even the idea of being "sober" (Greek *nephomen*) need not be taken in the literal sense of "intoxicated." In its context, "sober" is best understood metaphorically, meaning to be in control of oneself in a variety of circumstances. Use of alcohol would be one of these circumstances.

Simply put, the Christian manner of living is to be markedly different from that of someone who is not a Christian. The difference is to be as noticeable as that between light and dark, day and night, etc. Choices and options that are logical ones for non-Christians are not to be found in the life of the Christian. The difference comes from the allegiances and loyalties of the Christian. "We are not of the night, nor of darkness," Paul says in verse five. The NIV makes the translation more blunt, saying "we do not belong to the night or to the darkness."

Because "we are not of the night," Paul advises further spiritual preparedness so as to be ready when the Lord returns. The familiar Christian triad of "faith, hope, and love" is mentioned in verse eight, connected with military images of preparing for battle. A Roman soldier anticipating battle would have had as part of his uniform a breastplate and helmet to protect his vital organs from injury. A soldier would give a great amount of attention to the maintenance and care of these vital pieces of equipment, because they were an essential part of surviving a battle, protecting organs that are vital to life.

The heart and mind are also vital organs in the spiritual life, and a Christian does well to give as much attention (and more) to his spiritual armor as the soldier does to his physical armor. The Christian's "heart" or "soul" is to be protected by the breastplate of faith and love. *Faith* enables the Christian to see the world as God sees; *love* helps the Christian respond toward other persons (be they "neighbor" or "enemy") with the attitude of Jesus.

Similarly, the Christian's mind is to be protected by the helmet of "the hope of salvation." People today often use the word "hope" to describe their wish that something that seems unlikely to happen will actually come to pass. But in Christian terms, hope is the positive expectation of something good, grounded in the promises of God. *Hope* encourages Christians to have great confidence in the promise of salvation, in spite of all the unrighteousness in the world.

Keeping "the breastplate of faith and love, and as a helmet the hope of salvation" in good working order from the corrupting powers of "dark," "night," "sleep," and "drunkenness" will enable the Christian to not be "overtaken" by the return of the Lord. The believer that practices these qualities will be prepared for, and even be anticipating, that glorious day.

(5:9-11) For God did not appoint us to wrath, but to obtain salvation through our Lord Jesus Christ, who died for us, that whether we wake or sleep, we should live together with Him. Therefore comfort each other and edify one another, just as you also are doing.

Paul carefully alternates throughout the early part of 1 Thessalonians 5 the pronouns "they" and "them" (in verses 3 and 7) with "you and us" (in verses 4-6, 8-9)—to show that he did not envision the church remaining on earth during the time when the destruction (verse 3) which shall be revealed in "the day of the Lord" (verse 2) suddenly comes to pass.

For those who are not saved, the "day of the Lord" will be a day of wrath. Christians, however, will properly encourage each other in anticipation of that day, because they have been appointed for salvation.

As stated in the commentary on 1 Thessalonians 1:4 on the topic of election, God has always wanted a group of persons set apart for His special purposes. Christians have been appointed for those purposes. When Christ returns, all believers will live with Him. Those who have died, as well as those who are living at the time of the Lord's return—will experience life with God. Christians will live with Christ! These are truly words of comfort. Pass it on!

Chapter 5

INSTRUCTIONS ABOUT THE ORDER
OF THE CHURCH
1 Thessalonians 5:12-22

The final set of instructions Paul provides the Thessalonians can be grouped together under the heading "instructions about the order of the church." Paul's work in Thessalonica involved more than getting a group of persons together in one place. The work was to build the church. Because "the church" is not a building, that work involved gathering a group of people to be in relationship with God, and then encouraging those persons in their relationship with each other.

Along the way, there were bound to be difficulties on both points, some of which have already been addressed. In the last verses of chapter 5, Paul turns his attention directly to relationships in the church. In this world, people will not always get along with one another perfectly. Being "the church" involves a considerable investment in people because (among other reasons) human nature "rubs one another the wrong way" and is mistrustful of others' motives. The teaching in these verses serves to provide some "lubrication" for interpersonal relationships in the church.

A joy in these verses, however, is that they provide more than just general instruction about personal relationships in the church. A deeper examination reveals some indication as to the character of the gathered community of believers. What kind of persons are these Christians? In one sense, this entire section serves as commentary on 1 Thessalonians 5:19: "Do not quench the Spirit." How are believers to live together and faithfully be the church? How does the behavior of Christians differ from those who are not Christians? Paul provides instructions concerning a Christian view of leadership, relationships within the church, the spiritual life, and the church's ministry. Taken together, they provide helpful instructions on some practical aspects of the Christian life.

1. A Christian view of leadership (5:12-13)

The New Testament addresses the topic of leadership in at least three different ways. In some places, leadership is described in terms of *position*. The role of the apostle, deacon, or elder (to name a few) is the focus of these passages of Scripture. In other places, leadership is described in terms of *function*. These are the sections that detail the variety and use of spiritual gifts.

In these verses, Paul speaks of leadership in a third manner. Some in the Thessalonian church became leaders by virtue of the quality and quantity of their efforts in the new church. They were not necessarily appointed leaders; instead, they were leaders who were "rising to the top." Their potential to hold a *position* or demonstrate a particular *function* was being developed in their day to day labors for Christ and the church.

These verses are a window into the early stages of leadership development in the Thessalonian church. The Christians there were young in the faith, and Paul had not spent enough time with them to develop leadership to any great extent. Those who would lead by position or function were still in the making.

These verses show leadership "rising to the top." The discussion that follows will consider how the church today might allow leadership to "rise to the top" and also consider the idea of the *priesthood of all believers*.

(5:12-13) And we urge you, brethren, to recognize those who labor among you, and are over you in the Lord and admonish you, and to esteem them very highly in love for their work's sake. Be at peace among yourselves.

In any group of persons, a few individuals will be present who have leadership capability. These are persons who are willing to pitch in, who have a vision of how things might be in the future, and can share that vision with others so that many work toward a common goal. This was going on in Thessalonica. Certain persons were "laboring" diligently and effectively in the church there, both through hard work and by careful spiritual example. Others were naturally following these persons—following their example and trusting their opinions, and even listening to their admonishment.

These verses also suggest that the church was not without some measure of disagreement. This was not a perfect church. Already, Paul has mentioned their troubles with persecution (3:3-4); hinted that some may not have been working as hard as they might (4:11); and addressed their sorrow over those who have died (4:13-18).

Some tension may have existed between the leadership and the rest of the congregation. To help with these challenges, Paul "urges" the Thessalonians to both "recognize" and "esteem" these leaders. It may be too strong to say that Paul is taking the side of the leaders in some unspoken conflict or disagreement in the church, but he is clearly using his position of love and respect with the Thessalonians, to build these leaders up. By supporting the leadership and encouraging the church to treat those who labor in the ministry with the appropriate respect, Paul is giving them credibility as the leadership of the church.

Paul also instructs the church to "be at peace among

yourselves." Imagining why Paul would include this command is difficult, unless he suspected some lack of peace in the church. Perhaps those issues mentioned earlier caused the lack of peace. Again, it would be too much to say that there was open conflict among the Thessalonian church: Paul's practice was to deal with such conflict openly, as he did in his letters to the Galatians and Corinthians. Instead, the comments here are intended to give some guidance and direction to a group of new Christians working out their relationships with God and one another.

The instruction given here is sound teaching for every generation of Christians. It is human nature to be overly critical of the efforts of our brothers and sisters in the church. Rather than pitching in and working toward a common goal that will glorify God and strengthen the church, some choose to hold back their efforts and criticize those who are willing to get things done. Compounding the problem is the reality that many church disagreements concern issues that matter little in the long-term. All believers would do well to take Paul's admonitions to heart and set aside petty conflicts.

On a more positive note, these verses suggest what Anabaptists and Pietists have come to call *the priesthood of all believers*. Christians are filled with the Holy Spirit and can share God's grace with other persons. Leadership functions in the church are not reserved for a select few; instead, *all* are called and gifted in some manner to do the work of Christ. There is no hierarchy in the priesthood of all believers; instead, all persons are equal in God's sight. While some may be called to be "apostles" or "pastors," or may be gifted with one type of spiritual gift or another, all are to be used for building up the church.

In Anabaptist and Pietist circles, the idea of the priesthood of all believers was the understanding that led many congregations to practice the plural, unsalaried ministry. Certain men were called out of the local congregation to lead that congregation. Elders did not wear long robes or stand behind an elevated pulpit as a symbol of their position. Instead, they stood behind a table on the same level as the congregation, to deliver the message God had given to them for that particular situation.[26]

Because 1 Thessalonians is Paul's earliest epistle, these verses represent the earliest stages of leadership development in the church. And while it is well to affirm in the strongest way possible, the necessity for leadership by both position and function, it is helpful to consider if there is use for such "unofficial" leadership in the church today. How might leadership "rise to the top" to meet the abundance of need in the world today?

A strong emphasis on the priesthood of all believers in today's church will involve Christians focusing a great deal of time and effort outside the local church body. Instead of channeling all of their strongest leaders into church committees, some members should be encouraged to exercise their spiritual gifts as ambassadors for Christ, serving as missionaries in other parts of the world. Congregations who make the priesthood of all believers a high priority, and spent much of their time and resources for ministering outside the church, will excite the congregation and provide a strong witness to the world about them.

2. A Christian view of one another (5:14-15)

One of the clearest ways to distinguish the church from the world is in how those who are "weak" are treated. In this fallen world, it is normal for those persons who are weak to

---

[26]   Brethren Encyclopedia, *Priesthood of All Believers*, page 1057.

be marginalized, ignored, or openly abused. In the Scripture, however, both Old and New Testaments show God taking a special interest in those who are weak. Whether it is an Old Testament passage that describes God as a God who "administers justice for the fatherless and the widow, and loves the stranger, giving him food and clothing" (Deuteronomy 10:18), or a gospel passage showing Jesus actively being a friend of sinners—God is interested in the plight of those the world deems "weak." How this is to be displayed in the church is the focus of the next few verses.

(5:14-15) Now we exhort you, brethren, warn those who are unruly, comfort the fainthearted, uphold the weak, be patient with all. See that no one renders evil for evil to anyone, but always pursue what is good both for yourselves and for all.

Paul identifies three categories of persons who are at risk for being marginalized: the unruly, the fainthearted, and the weak. Some would see them as "the problem children of the church." What is the reaction of the church to these persons in their midst?

The first reaction concerns the *"unruly."* The precise translation of the Greek word *ataktos* is the matter of some scholarly discussion. Some translations tend to agree with the NKJV translation of "unruly." Others translate the word as "idle." In its essence, the word refers to the situation of a person not behaving in a normally expected fashion. In this sense, the *Amplified Bible* best captures the meaning by translating this phrase "admonish those who are out of line." Both "unruly" and "idle" are examples of being "out of line."

What specific situation did Paul have in mind when he wrote concerning those who were "unruly"? Other comments in this letter provide some clues. In 1 Thessalonians 4:11, Paul instructs the church to "lead a quiet life, to mind your own business, and to work with your own hands, as we commanded you, that you may walk properly toward those who are outside, and that you may lack nothing." Looking forward to 2 Thessalonians 3:6-15, Paul instructs those who were intentionally not working to get to work. It has been suggested that some in Thessalonica were so anticipating the return of Christ that they had quit their work and were "sponging" off the church while they waited. It does not take much imagination to see how such behavior might be described as either "unruly" or "idle." Such persons needed to be admonished to behave appropriately and honor the teaching of 1 Thessalonians 5:1-11.

The second group of persons is identified as *"the fainthearted."* Paul has also identified two reasons why people might be fainthearted. In 1 Thessalonians 3:2-4, Paul gives strong encouragement to the church in the face of persecution, to which he says, "we are appointed." Persecution is not something North American Christians can speak of with any authority, yet the example of persecution is found in Anabaptist-Pietist heritage. Clearly the possibility of persecution would weigh heavily on some persons, and they would need to be comforted.

The second reason why people might be fainthearted is seen in 1 Thessalonians 4:13. As discussed in that section, the death of believers before Christ's return was a matter of great concern to some of the Thessalonians. Paul addressed this situation at some length; now it was up to the church to encourage and comfort those grieving persons.

Third, Paul instructs the Thessalonians to "uphold *the weak.*" There is nothing unique about the Greek word translated "weak" to indicate any specific type of weakness. Paul's comments in 1 Thessalonians 4:1-8 on the topic of sexual purity, however, could be the weakness Paul has in mind. As persons left behind old patterns of belief and behavior, there would naturally be a struggle with these old ways. Patterns and addictions are not easily broken, and old addictions and moral struggles will continue in the new life in Christ. Believers should expect that life in Christ will bring victory in such battles, but must not discount the need to carefully prepare for the battles.

The church should be a place where persons are upheld in their struggle with sin. Rather than ignoring such people, the church should support them in their growth toward more mature Christian living.

The fourth and final group of people who are often marginalized in the church are those who have *caused* hurt. When the actions of one church member create division in the church, he often finds other Christians turning against him. Conflicts become battles with "winners" and "losers." Persons in the same congregation stop speaking to one another, openly criticize other members, and encourage others to take sides in the conflict. Such behavior is anything but being "patient with all."

Certainly, conflict and hurt feelings within the church must be dealt with in an appropriate manner. "Sweeping things under the rug" may seem like the best strategy in the short term, but in the end only encourages strife and discord in the fellowship. Conflict must be dealt with openly and properly. Part of an appropriate response to conflict is seeking to maintain the integrity and spiritual atmosphere of the church while dealing with the hurt. Rather than encouraging persons to take sides, the leadership of the church must work to maintain the health and stability of the church in addition to working with persons as they sort out the conflict. In such ways Christians "pursue what is good both for yourselves and for all."

3. A Christian view of the spiritual life (5:16-18)

In these verses Paul turns his attention to life in the Spirit. The Christian lives with a vision of eternal life, expecting Jesus' return at any moment, yet busy working for the kingdom. The promises of Scripture provide great hope for the believer that ought to affect every part of the Christian life. No matter what a Christian faces in life, there is a hope that is beyond this world, which colors and shapes Christian living.

Even with this great hope, however, there will be times when the believer is sorely tested. Those trials may take the form of persecution because of faith in Christ, as was the Thessalonians' experience. Trials may also take the form of an unexpected tragedy or accident that happens for no apparent reason. In such times, being built up and encouraged by faith in Christ is a challenge indeed.

How is the Christian to combine this great future hope with the joys, concerns, celebrations, and sufferings of earthly life? The simple instructions in the next verses provide an answer.

(5:16-18) Rejoice always, pray without ceasing, in everything give thanks; for this is the will of God in Christ Jesus for you.

The first comment to be made concerning these three verses concerns the last phrase of verse 18, "for this is the will of God in Christ Jesus for you." This phrase clearly refers to the three points of instruction that precede it, not merely the last.

These verses, like others in the epistle to the Thessalonians, express "God's will." Wondering about God's will is not unusual for Christians. There will be times when believers will need to diligently pursue God's will for their lives. For those times when they are inclined to think that doing God's will is only for the "super-spiritual," the instructions here provide a different perspective. Doing God's will is possible for anyone willing to pursue God in some surprisingly ordinary ways.

These verses express God's will for everyday living. The three straightforward commands given in these verses are excellent disciplines that can be used to cultivate spiritual depth in the life of a believer. They are especially to be commended to the new believer.

A second preliminary comment concerning these commands will be made here and expanded in later sections. The instructions in these verses are present imperatives (commands) in the Greek language. It would be accurate to translate these verses "keep on rejoicing," "keep on praying without ceasing," "keep on giving thanks." The nature of the grammar and the actual commands themselves point out that these are not commands merely for the sake of commanding; neither are they offered in the sense of "do this or else." Instead, Paul is encouraging the Thessalonians to "keep on" practicing certain qualities of the Christian life. Keep on doing them until they become habit and custom.

When persons who are not members of our local church look at the life of our church, what do they say? Are our fellowships known as "rejoicing churches"? Do outsiders look at our congregations and say "That church is always praying"? Have we ever been "accused" of being "the most thankful people on the face of the earth?" Such are Paul's intentions.

(5:16) Rejoice always,

The first command Paul provides concerning life in the Spirit is to "rejoice always." Joy is one quality of life by which the believer should be known.

There is much in this world that is negative and angry.

People are confronted daily with anger expressed through violence. Much popular music and dress is focused on rage or the glorification of sin. With the long litany of complaints one may have with this world, how can anyone be expected to "rejoice always?"

To properly understand "joy," it must first be distinguished from "happiness." Happiness is an emotion tied to whatever one is experiencing right now. It comes and goes depending on the circumstances. Because some life experiences are difficult or tragic, it would be highly inappropriate to insist that someone "be happy always." God has given human beings a full range of emotions, and there is legitimate need for each. A quick glance through the Scripture shows that even God is not "happy" all the time.

Joy differs from happiness because joy is not an emotion. Joy is a fruit of the Spirit (see Galatians 5:22). It is a product of life in Christ. As a believer walks with Christ and is shaped in holiness by the Holy Spirit, joy will be one of several results. Because joy is a fruit of the Spirit and not an emotion, it is not tied to our present circumstances and feelings. Circumstances will come and go. Joy is constant because it is grounded in the fact that God is working in believers' lives whatever their circumstances. Whatever they may be experiencing at any given moment is evidence of God at work. This is cause for joy.

Three times in 1 Thessalonians, before this point, Paul refers to "joy." A glance at these will provide a fuller meaning for the source of joy. He speaks of "having received the word in much affliction, with *joy* of the Holy Spirit." (1 Thessalonians 1:6). Again, he says, "For what is our hope, or *joy*, or crown of rejoicing? Is it not even you in the presence of our Lord Jesus Christ at His coming? For you are our glory and *joy*." (1 Thessalonians 2:19-20). And on one other occasion, Paul says, "For what thanks can we render to God for you, for all the *joy* with which we rejoice for your sake before our God" (1 Thessalonians 3:9).

In each of these circumstances, Paul's joy comes from the fact that God is at work in the lives of the Thessalonians. Whether that work be accepting the gospel in times of trial, or being formed into a faithful body of believers—God is at work in these people, and the evidence of that work brings Paul much joy. Though his present circumstances are not what he would wish (his words in chapters two and three do not show happiness) Paul can still feel great joy over the work God is doing. Such should be the attitude of each Christian, for God is still at work. "Keep on being joyful," one might say, "because God keeps on working in your life!"

To summarize, then, joy is a deep, inner radiance of the soul that results from a harmonized relationship between the believer and God.

(5:17) pray without ceasing,

Instruction and encouragement concerning prayer should be warmly received in the life of the church. In an age where war, economic challenges, corporate downsizing and declining morals are the norm, "Keep on praying!" should be echoed from the pulpits in all congregations.

Sadly, however, the opposite seems to be the case. Except for the "pastoral prayer" in Sunday worship services, prayer receives less attention than it should be receiving among Christians today. Surveys consistently show that even pastors average only minutes per day in prayer.

It could be that the affluence of North American culture is the culprit in a deficient prayer life. With the wealth that abounds in this society, it is easy to act as if one does not need prayer. Why pray for daily bread when there is an extra car in the garage? Why pray for clothing when there are extra clothes in the closet? Why pray for health or healing with the advanced medical technology available today?

Those who "keep on praying" understand life differently. They understand that these verses are not an instruction to pray 24 hours out of each day, but are instead an invitation to be led by the Spirit. The church is not an institution run by men and women, but a body of believers seeking to follow God's will in a particular time and place.

Life in the Spirit does not mean passively following a distant and unknowable God, but pursuing a relationship with the One who first loved us and knows and loves us better than we can ever know and love ourselves. How is a Christian to know God's will without taking time to know God? Such knowledge only comes from spending time with God in prayer, and by doing this we follow Paul's instruction to "keep on praying!"

Churches in some parts of the world, especially where Christianity is either disfavored or faces outright persecution, know the power of prayer. Richard Foster provides a challenging example of prayer that comes from Christians in South Korea who attend the Myong-Song Presbyterian church:

> This is a group that began about ten years ago with forty people, and today twelve thousand gather each morning for three prayer meetings—at 4:00 a.m., 5:00 a.m. and 6:00 a.m. Jung-Oh [a member of the church] explained to me that they must shut the doors at 4:00 a.m. to begin the first service, and so if people arrive a little late, they must wait until the 5:00 a.m. meeting. Then he added, "This is a problem in my country because it gets cold in the winter! So everyone brings a little pot of tea or coffee to keep warm while they wait for the next service." This is organized, corporate, intercessory prayer.[27]

---

[27]   Richard J. Foster, *Prayer*, page 198.

(5:18) in everything give thanks;

The instruction to "keep on being thankful" concludes the section of "life in the Spirit." It is perhaps human nature to view life pessimistically. For many persons, the glass seems to be "half empty." Everyone has challenges in life, to be sure. Yet a valuable spiritual exercise is to occasionally stop and list everything in life for which one is thankful. Instead of complaining about another person with whom it is difficult to get along, stop and give thanks for that person's positive qualities. When the church "down the road" seems to have everything going in its favor, stop and give thanks for all the spiritual gifts that are available among the membership of the home church. When facing a difficult situation in life, give thanks to God—not *for* the circumstances, but that God will work *through* and *in* the circumstances.

Earlier in the commentary (1 Thessalonians 4:1-2), Paul wrote of his desire for the Thessalonians to "abound more and more" (4:1). It is nearly impossible for believers to abound when all that they see is what is wrong. Complaining, criticizing, and having a pessimistic attitude will rob the believer of joy. Christians do well to develop the spiritual discipline of giving thanks. Such a practice will enable each Christian to see the abundance of blessings given from God, and to see God at work in the world. This (along with rejoicing and praying) is part of God's will for the believer, an essential quality of the Christian life.

4. A Christian view of the church's ministry (5:19-22)

The final instructions in this section of the letter are a simple list of commands to help the church in its ministry. This set of instructions is similar to those that have come before, in that they are simple commands that are straightforward in meaning. The purpose of this section is to help the church in its ministry: discerning the leading of the Holy Spirit, and enabling Christians to live holy lives.

As with all of Scripture, however, understanding the instruction and putting it into practice are often two very different things. The challenge with these particular instructions is that they are very Spirit-oriented. It is possible for sincere believers to disagree on what the Spirit might be saying at a particular moment. No testing method is provided, and what qualifies as "evil" (verse 22) always seems open for debate. Human emotions and wishes get in the way of Spirit-living here as much as anywhere.

This should not be cause for despair. Living in the blessings of the Spirit is possible for the church. Such living will not be easy and will take much time dedicated to prayer, study of the Scripture, and discernment. The instructions provided here—when placed in the context of those who are mature Christians committed to one another, the local church, and Spirit-living—provide much help in having a faithful ministry.

(5:19) Do not quench the Spirit.

The Christians at Corinth, at times, were apparently too noisy and informal, and were instructed to do things "decently and in order" (1 Corinthians 14:40). The Thessalonians may have been more cold and formal, resulting in a quenching of the Spirit. There is a balance between order and an opportunity for the Spirit to work.

As was stated in the opening of this chapter, it is possible to see verse 19 as the linchpin to this entire section. If a local church were made up of lazy, disrespectful, spiteful, cold Christians who never prayed or gave thanks for anything—yet believed and did almost everything—it is difficult to see how the Spirit could reach such a hard-hearted lot of believers. Such Christians are like the husband, whose wife described him to a group of friends as "a model husband." The husband was impressed until he got home and found the definition of model in the dictionary: "a small imitation of the real thing." Faithful application of the instructions on either side of verse 19 will go a long way toward cultivating a depth of faith that can be used in a mighty way.

How do Christians avoid quenching the Spirit? Some ways are—to put into practice the commands of Scripture; to discover their spiritual gifts; to understand the fruit of the Spirit and to seek to bear all the fruit described in Galatians 5; it is also important to be diligent in worship and prayer.

Mennonite writer, Myron Augsburger, gives another answer to this question. He likens being attentive to the Spirit to being a good conversationalist. To share in engaging conversation with another person, one must be a good listener. The same is true with life in the Spirit. If believers want to know what the Spirit is saying, then they must *listen.*[28] Prayer must include times for listening to God. Scripture must be allowed to speak on its own. Worship services should include times of listening and discernment. As Christians develop the habits of listening to the Spirit, they will find the Spirit quite ready to speak.

(5:20) Do not despise prophecies.

There is some degree of confusion about the nature of prophecy in the world today. When people mention the word "prophecy," they often think this refers to "foretelling," that is, predicting the future. This nearly always includes beliefs about the end of the age. The Scripture does contain much prophecy that fits into this category. One need only think about the many Old Testament prophecies about the Mes-

---

[28]   Myron S. Augsburger, *Quench Not the Spirit*, page 50.

siah, and the many prophecies concerning Christ's return to see that this is true.

There is also a second function of prophecy that is quite common in Scripture. This is prophecy as "forth-telling." This use of prophecy consists of a person delivering a Spirit-inspired message intended for the people of God. It can be an indictment of sin or a word or teaching addressing a local situation. In either case, this type of prophecy is God's word to God's people.

There are at least two reasons why persons might be inclined to "despise prophecies." First, there are those who see the "foretelling" type of prophecy as too open for interpretation, too difficult to understand, or just not relevant to living in the here and now. There have been so many false prophets predicting the "end of the world" that many are simply not interested in hearing about the end times. In a world of some who are pre-millennialist and others who are post-millennialist, many choose to be "pan-millennialist," believing that it will all "pan out in the end."

In context of this passage, however, it seems likely that Paul is referring to the second function of prophecy, that of the "forth-telling" type. The church may have been unwilling to hear and accept this type of prophecy because it was challenging some of its shortcomings and sin, as has been discussed earlier in the commentary. Prophecy is always challenging because it is difficult to think that one's own lifestyle might be contributing to some injustice in the community or the world. We like *not to think that our own behavior* within the church might be quenching the Spirit. The call to repentance is not always a welcome message. Church of the Brethren pastor Paul Grout offers some prophetic words on this point when he says, "New life begins with repentance. Most people in the church agree that repentance is needed and will gladly point out people for whom it is necessary."[29]

Christians should not despise prophecy because it is one method that God uses to speak to the church today. At times, hearing prophecy is like receiving a serious medical diagnosis. Hearing it is not easy. Nevertheless, healing and recovery can only begin after one diagnoses a problem and chooses a course of treatment. On this point, what is true physically is also true spiritually. While prophetic words are not often easy to hear, they are words from a loving God who seeks the best interests of His followers. They are despised at the risk of our spiritual well being.

(5:21) Test all things; hold fast what is good.

In the context of the passage, the command of verse 21 refers to the instructions of verses 19 and 20. "All things" refers to both not quenching the Spirit and not despising prophecies. Such matters are to be tested. The reason is that confusing the words of fallible humans with those of an infallible God is easy. People often hear what they want to hear, not what they need to hear. Discerning between human thoughts and intentions and those of the Spirit is not an easy task, even for mature Christians. Calling persons to repentance over a specific action is not an easy thing to do. Sadly, there is always the temptation of forcing one's own will on persons under the guise of the Spirit.

Paul instructs the Thessalonians first to "test all things." All workings of the Spirit, all words of prophecy, are to be tested. But how? Paul offers no specific guidelines. A few common sense guidelines would be to first, consider the speaker. Are the words coming from those who are "over

---

[29]   Paul Grout, "Into the Future: Remedies for a Church that Has Stopped Being Alive," *Messenger*, May 2001, page 18.

you in the Lord and admonish you" (verse 12), those whose manner of living continually indicates a spiritual depth and trustworthiness?

Second, does that which is offered in the name of the Spirit agree with the character of the Spirit-inspired written word? If the "prophecy" offered is contrary to Scripture, then it must be rejected. To hold this position is not to say that God does not do new things. The Spirit is at work in the particulars of current situations as much as in those of Paul's congregations. In either case, the character of the Spirit will always agree with the written Word.

Third, does the teaching or prophecy build up the body of believers, either by providing helpful instruction or challenging sin? This also is an indicator of the work of the Spirit.

The church should "hold fast" to such words. The Greek word translated "hold fast" means to "keep in memory," "retain faithfully," and "guard."[30] All of us tend to "hold fast" to those things that are dear to us, for example, certain memories of loved ones and some especially prized possessions. Such should be the attitude of Christians toward the authentic words of the Spirit.

(5:22) Abstain from every form of evil.

The final instruction in the category "a Christian view of the church's ministry" is to abstain from every form of evil. This instruction reminds the believer that the actions of the church—both individual members and the church as a whole—reflect on the church and the character of Christ. The lives of Christians and the church as a whole are to be clearly different from the world. Christians claim an alle-

---

[30]   William F. Arndt and F. Wilbur Gingrich, *A Greek-English Lexicon of the New Testament.* The word is *katecho,* page 422-423.

giance that is higher than nation, business, and even family. The ultimate allegiance is to Christ.

As such, the Christian is to abstain from every form of evil, and must simply not become involved, even in what may be considered by some to be borderline activities. Albert Barnes, in his notes on the New Testament, says in essence that there are many things which in themselves may not appear to be positively wrong, but which are considered to be wrong by large and respectable portions of the community. Thus, for believers to do them, would be regarded as inconsistent and improper.

A valuable part of the church's ministry is helping people identify their own participation in evil, and then encouraging them to escape from those kinds of conduct.

Chapter 6

CONCLUSION
1 Thessalonians 5:23-28

The conclusion to the first epistle to the Thessalonians follows the standard letter writing format of the day. The technical description for these verses is "final greeting and farewell." For usage in Christian study and worship, however, it would be better to call this section "benediction and blessing." These are more than polite words. They are intended for spiritual benefit.

For purposes of discussion, these verses will be divided into two sections. They also function nicely as a unit, and believers may wish to make these into a prayer of their own, substituting the name of an individual or congregation into the verses as is appropriate.

1. The promises of God to faithful believers (5:23-24)

Paul's words in these two verses are best understood as a "blessing." Much the way a loving parent desires to see certain qualities develop in the lives of his children, Paul wishes to see certain characteristics develop in the lives of the Thessalonians. Many of these have been discussed at length already in the letter.

Here, Paul offers his blessing to the Thessalonians. Having grown up in a Jewish home and trained in Jewish rabbinical schools, Paul understood that the blessing he offers is "inspired" when given in harmony with God's desires.[31] Paul believed the words of this blessing had the

---

[31]   *New International Dictionary of Old Testament Theology and Exegesis, volume 1,* word # 1385, pages 760-761.

power to bring about what was desired, and thus, they are a matter of deep spiritual concern. [32]

(5:23-24) Now may the God of peace Himself sanctify you completely; and may your whole spirit, soul, and body be preserved blameless at the coming of our Lord Jesus Christ. He who calls you is faithful, who also will do it.

a. God is a God of peace. The first characteristic of this blessing is a statement of the character of God. God is a God of peace. For those raised in Anabaptist circles, this part of God's character comes as no surprise. Their forebears have long emphasized the teachings of Jesus to "turn the other cheek" and "love your enemies." With war, violence, and terrorism an ever present reality in the present world, Christians in the historic peace churches have a powerful witness to the character of God.

Christians do well, however, to see "peace" as more than the absence of conflict. Having peace among persons who are prone to violence is an essential part of the peace witness. But it is not the only part. Both the Old Testament word *shalom* and the New Testament word *eirene* (both translated "peace") refer to more than the absence of conflict. They refer to the presence of "wholeness" or "having enough." The idea is captured rather completely in 1 Kings 4:25: "And Judah and Israel dwelt safely, each man under his vine and fig tree, from Dan as far as Beersheba, all the days of Solomon." Both the absence of conflict ("dwelt safely") and having enough ("each man under his vine and fig tree") are seen in this verse. God is a God of peace, and desires that these qualities be reflected in the lives of all persons.

---

[32]   The Old Testament contains numerous examples of this concept of blessing. The classic example of this way of thinking about a blessing is found in Isaac's blessings of Esau and Jacob in Genesis 27.

b. As one is sanctified, he will reflect that peace. The second part of the blessing follows from the first, and is intended for God's people. The meaning of "sanctified" has already been discussed in this commentary: God desires that His followers be holy and reflect aspects of godliness in their living. Paul's desire is that the Thessalonians be sanctified "completely," that is, all aspects of their living will reflect godly values. One of these is peace.

In keeping with what was stated above, Paul intends that there not be open conflict among believers, either in the home or in the church, nor directed against the world. The peace of Christ that should be on display in the lives of Christians will also indicate the quality of wholeness.

In today's society, there are many indications that believers do not experience "wholeness" to the level they might. People today work more to spend more. Days are often non-stop from beginning to end, filled with stressful jobs (made even more stressful with the added responsibilities from corporate downsizing). Children are overly scheduled, often going from school to ball practice, or lessons of some sort each night of the week. Husbands and wives are often "ships passing in the night" as they juggle these demands. When leisure time does arrive, it is often spent in front of the television, which does not provide the type of relaxation persons need.

It is certainly true that life's demands cannot be avoided. Something will always provide stress; that is a reality of living. But the church today would do well to understand the concept of "wholeness" and encourage members of their congregations to examine their lives and make changes so they might experience the blessing of peace and wholeness that God desires, even saying "no" to what might be good things, so as not to be over-scheduled. Author M. Shawn

Copeland says it this way:

> Throughout Christian history, it has been clear that Christianity is not a spectator activity. Tough decisions and persistent effort are required of those who seek lives that are whole and holy. If we are to grow in faithful living, we need to renounce the things that choke off the fullness of life that God intended for us, and we must follow through on our commitments to pray, to be conscientious, and to be in mutually supportive relations with other faithful persons. These acts take self-discipline. We must learn the practice of saying no to that which crowds God out and yes to a way of life that makes space for God.[33]

c. Humans are not compartmentalized beings. In contemporary Western culture, people often act as if spirit, soul, and body are separate aspects of living. *"Spirit"* is often seen as the essence of a human being, that part of individuals which describes who they are. This may be their love for other persons, their joyful personality, their dedication and devotion. *"Soul"* is identified with the more spiritual aspects of living, that part of a person which is inclined toward God. *"Body"* is the physical part of living.

Finding that these three aspects of living are treated differently is common among persons. Some may have strongly developed "souls," in that they are quite dedicated to the church and religious things, but have abrasive spirits, or do not take care of their bodies. Others may be dedicated to caring for their bodies through healthy living, and not give their "souls" any attention at all.

Here, Paul identifies all three as receivers of blessing from the God of peace. All three aspects of human living—spirit, soul and body—are intended to be preserved blameless. The Christian "spirit" will reflect godly qualities.

---

[33] M. Shawn Copeland, "Saying Yes and Saying No," in *Practicing Our Faith: A Way of Life for Searching People*, page 60.

The "soul" will be kept in tune with the leading of the Holy Spirit. The body, while subject to disease, will be cared for as a reflection of faith in God. Persons who are over-stressed, running from one commitment to the next, are typically not able to keep these three aspects of living in balance with one another. A good spiritual discipline for living in today's world would be to give direct attention to all three aspects of living, that each may be "preserved blameless."

d. We may count on God's promises and power. Paul's blessing concludes with a second description of God's character. Not only is God the "God of peace," God is also "faithful" (verse 24). As described here in Thessalonians, Christian living is not an easy task. There will always be challenges and questions with which sincere Christians will struggle long and hard. Keeping spirit, soul, and body in balance with one another is a continual challenge.

Nevertheless, for those times when everything seems confused and out of balance, Paul's blessing reminds all who will take heed, that God is faithful. God will not abandon his followers in times of difficulty. Instead, God will "do" what is promised. God can be relied upon. As Paul says in a later epistle, "He who has begun a good work in you will complete it until the day of Jesus Christ" (Philippians 1:6).

2. Concluding wishes and prayer (5:25-28)

The final verses of 1 Thessalonians are short, easily understood statements that will require little comment.

(5:25-28) Brethren, pray for us. Greet all the brethren with a holy kiss. I charge you by the Lord that this epistle be read to all the holy brethren. The grace of our Lord Jesus Christ be with you. Amen.

Paul begins by requesting prayer for himself and the other apostles (verse 25). Imagining any number of reasons why Paul might desire prayer is easy: for his own struggles, for the hard work of preaching the gospel and planting churches, for his own health, and for the particular challenges of being a teacher. This request for prayer also encourages the Thessalonians to see outside their own particular situation and identify with the needs of other persons. A helpful spiritual exercise for Christians, either individually or as a group, would be to identify those in positions of leadership in the church, and list challenges particular to their situation, then commit those persons to prayer.

The second instruction in these verses is to greet fellow church members with a holy kiss (verse 26). A kiss on the cheek among persons of the same gender was a common practice in New Testament times, and continues to this day as well. It is not commonly seen in Western culture, although greeting friends with a kiss on the cheek is not completely unheard of, either.

From the time of the early church, down through the history of Christianity, the holy kiss has been attested to as the standard form of greeting among Christians. It is commanded several times in the New Testament.[34] Throughout generations of Christianity, believers exchanged the holy kiss in greeting, at baptism, and at the Lord's Supper. It is a heartfelt expression of Christian love.[35]

An equally important part of this verse, however, is the command to "greet one another." The bonds of love in the church are not to be neglected. If the congregation is too busy running from this meeting to that on Sunday mornings and does not have time to greet one another, something is amiss. Likewise, if feelings among members of the con-

---

[34] Romans 16:16; 1 Corinthians 16:20; 2 Corinthians 13:12; 1 Peter 5:14.
[35] Kiss, Holy. *Brethren Encyclopedia*, pages 698-699.

gregation have become strained to the point where greeting one another is avoided, then there is a problem in the church that needs careful attention.

Some will ask if the holy kiss should still be practiced in the church today. In many congregations, the holy kiss is reserved for Love Feast and communion services. But a faithful, straightforward application of these verses leads one to the conclusion that members of the church today should greet one another with the holy kiss as a matter of regular practice. The "holy kiss" can be a very meaningful greeting, one that will distinguish greetings among Christians from the world in general.[36]

The third instruction in these verses is for this letter to be read "to all the holy brethren" (verse 27). While the particular words of this letter were generated by specific situations in Thessalonica, the teaching is relevant for all Christians in churches today.

Finally, Paul finishes where he began, wishing "grace" to be with all of the Thessalonians (verse 28). Grace is what has changed the Thessalonians from objects of wrath into God's precious children, designed for good works in the kingdom of God. May the grace of God be with us all. Amen.

---

[36] Some, however, see Paul bringing the common practice of "the greeting of the day" into the life of the church. They would suggest that a common application in our day would be for believers to greet one another with a "holy handshake" or a "holy hug."

REVIEW QUESTIONS
1 Thessalonians

1. How do we understand ourselves as the church? How does our understanding of church as a body of believers—and not our building or program—affect our mission? our relationships with one another? the way we study the Bible? (1 Thessalonians 1:1)

2. Review the ten different "signs of authenticity" in this chapter. How are each of these at work in your life, and the life of your congregation? Which are stronger? Which are weaker? (1 Thessalonians 1:1-10).

3. In 2:7-12, Paul lists four qualities that he, Silas, and Timothy displayed among the Thessalonians: they were like a nursing mother, they gave of themselves, they were like a father, and they invited the church to faithful living. Think about the pastors (or other church leaders) you have known. How have these qualities been on display in their lives? How are they on display in your own (even if you do not have a leadership role in the church)?

4. In his commentary on 1 and 2 Thessalonians, professor Michael Holmes says the following: "We might ask ourselves why we are not experiencing the 'trials' that Paul assumes here will be the experience of believers. Three possible reasons spring to mind: (1) We have isolated ourselves in a Christian subculture (dare I say 'ghetto') of some sort; (2) we are the beneficiaries of fortunate circumstances; or (3) we are not really serious about our commitment to the gospel and its values".[37] Consider this quotation in light of 1 Thessalonians 3:3-4, and the exposition in this commentary.

---

[37] Michael W. Holmes, *1 & 2 Thessalonians, NIV Application Commentary*, page 110.

5.   In considering Paul's prayer in 1 Thessalonians 3:11-13, are there times when we are guilty of either expecting God to do all the work while we sit idly by? Are there times when we are guilty of neglecting to ask for God's help and instead press on in our own strength?

6.   In what ways has God's grace enabled you to "abound." How have you exceeded your own expectations in Christian living? (From 1 Thessalonians 4:1-2)

7.   Have you ever considered the fact that you can please God? How does this understanding change your relationship with God? (1 Thessalonians 4:1-2)

8.   How can you relate to being "taught by God"? (1 Thessalonians 4:9-10)

9.   What hopes, beliefs, and concerns do you have concerning the rapture and the return of Christ? Does this give you hope? (1 Thessalonians 4:13-18)

10.   What is the difference between happiness and joy? How do you understand God to be working in your life at this moment? Does that provide you joy? (1 Thessalonians 5:16)

11.   What experiences do you have with prophecy, either sharing words of prophecy or hearing words of prophecy that described your life? Does your local congregation value prophecy, and make room for it in worship? (1 Thessalonians 5:20)

12.   In what ways are you experiencing "peace" and "wholeness" in your life? What might need to change for you to experience the full measure of God's blessings of peace? (1 Thessalonians 5:23)

COMMENTARY
ON
2 THESSALONIANS

INTRODUCTION TO 2 THESSALONIANS

Second Thessalonians takes a common sense approach to some very real problems facing a sincere group of Christians. Written very shortly after the first letter to the Thessalonians, this second letter discusses many issues handled in the first letter. In doing so, Paul, Silvanus, and Timothy go beyond the first letter by giving additional teaching and instruction on some of the more significant challenges facing this young congregation. Modern readers will find that the issues facing the Thessalonian Christians are similar to those facing today's Christians.

Most of what was written in the Introduction to 1 Thessalonians is directly applicable here. A few additional issues, however, need to be mentioned with this letter.

1. Letter writing style

Paul has followed the standard letter writing style of the day in 2 Thessalonians. Dividing the letter in this fashion yields the following sections: a "prescript" identifying the senders (1:1a) and the recipients (1:1b); greeting (1:1c); prayer wish or thanksgiving (1:2-12); the body of the letter (2:1—3:15); final greeting and farewell (3:16-18). Second Thessalonians is unique in that it has a double farewell (3:16 and 3:17-18).

2. Authorship and date of writing

Most biblical scholars take the position that the apostle Paul wrote 2 Thessalonians (with the assistance of Silvanus and Timothy, one of whom may have served as scribe) very shortly after 1 Thessalonians. It is often assumed that 1 Thessalonians was written approximately in the year 51 AD, and that 2 Thessalonians was written approximately six months later.

Those persons doing wider study into 2 Thessalonians will likely find some scholars who identify this as a *pseudonymous* letter, meaning an unknown person wrote this epistle in the name of Paul. Scholars who say this generally hold that the letter was written many years after 1 Thessalonians. The position of this commentary, however, is that Paul wrote this letter shortly after the letter known as 1 Thessalonians.

3. Similarities between 1 and 2 Thessalonians

The main similarities between these two letters occur in chapters 1 and 3. Chapter 1 is of the standard greeting style, and provides further blessings and encouragement to these Christians. Chapter 3 continues treatment of the laziness problem that existed in the congregation. Because the language is stronger here, one may assume that Paul's instructions in 1 Thessalonians did not solve this problem.

Because of the amount of similar material in these two letters, the approach of this commentary will be as follows:

First, passages from 2 Thessalonians that are *identical* to those found in 1 Thessalonians will be handled by referring the reader to the appropriate section of 1 Thessalonians. For example, the phrase "grace and peace to you" occurs both in 1 Thessalonians 1:1 and 2 Thessalonians 1:2. This phrase will not be discussed again in this commentary.

Second, passages in 2 Thessalonians that are *similar* to those found in 1 Thessalonians will be treated in the necessary depth with ample reference to relevant passages in the first epistle.

Finally, new material will be given full treatment in the manner of the commentary on 1 Thessalonians.

Chapter 7

FURTHER ENCOURAGEMENT TO
PERSECUTED BELIEVERS
2 Thessalonians 1:1-12

A short period of time (perhaps several months) has passed since Paul wrote the letter of 1 Thessalonians. In the time since the sending of that letter, more news has come to Paul concerning the life and faith of the Thessalonian Christians. Much of what he heard was good news, and is reflected in the joyful encouragement found in this letter. As much as 1 Thessalonians chapter 1 addressed "signs of authenticity," the encouraging words of 2 Thessalonians chapter 1 are possible because of the "evidence of authenticity" in the Thessalonians' lives.

Still, not all of the news from the church has been good. The reports of ongoing persecution are troubling, and some believers appear to be wondering about God's sense of justice. Does their suffering mean that God is unjust? Why do the righteous suffer and the unrighteous prosper? The same question is part of the discussion in the book of Job found in the Old Testament.

These are questions that Christians have asked since Jesus' day. While Paul's words here might not serve as answers to our specific questions, his comments are helpful to those searching for answers to life's painful challenges in our day. For those who wonder why God allows bad things to happen to good people, at least part of an answer can be found here: bad things, when they take the form of suffering for faith, are an indicator of authentic faith. In such circumstances, suffering does not come as a result of God's disapproval; rather, it is the result of the world's disapproval.

1. Introduction (1:1-2)

Paul begins this epistle with a prescript and greeting, in keeping with the standard letter writing format of the day.

(1:1-2) Paul, Silvanus, and Timothy, To the church of the Thessalonians in God our Father and the Lord Jesus Christ: Grace to you and peace from God our Father and the Lord Jesus Christ.

The church at Thessalonica was established on Paul's second missionary journey. Silvanus (Silas) and Timothy were co-senders of this epistle because they had worked with Paul at Thessalonica. Barnabas was with Paul on the first missionary journey, but he had been replaced by Silas.

It is helpful to note in these introductory words that Paul says the welcome is from "God *our* Father." This says something about the sense of relationship that Paul felt with God. God is not some distant Father who is completely unknowable and unapproachable; neither is God a generic deity that can be made to suit a variety of purposes. God is *our* Father and can be known and worshiped "in spirit and in truth" (John 4:23). This kind of relationship with God was evident in Paul's first letter to the Thessalonians, and is evident here as well.

2. Evidence of authentic faith (1:3-4)

Paul was never one to be stingy with praise when it was appropriately given. He had learned that the Thessalonian Christians have a growing faith in spite of their trials, and for this he gives thanks.

In the Greek text, verses 3-10 are one sentence. While writing such long sentences was proper in Greek, the rules of English grammar dictate shorter sentences. One task of translation is determining where to break longer Greek sentences into shorter English ones.

Verses 3-4 function well as one unit, and many translations recognize this by treating these two verses as either one or two sentences. The NKJV translation follows the longer sentence structure of the Greek. This commentary will treat verses 3-4 as one unit.

(1:3-4) We are bound to thank God always for you, brethren, as it is fitting, because your faith grows exceedingly, and the love of every one of you all abounds toward each other, so that we ourselves boast of you among the churches of God for your patience and faith in all your persecutions and tribulations that you endure,

First Thessalonians 3 describes Paul's great concern for these beloved friends. The cause of Paul's concern is whether or not the Thessalonians could weather the storm of trouble. Paul's prayer in 1 Thessalonians 3:11-13 is that he could have a continued role in their faith development and that their love for one another would continue to grow in the midst of trials.

This letter is evidence of answered prayer. Much of what Paul had hoped for in his prayer wishes in 1 Thessalonians 3 was being experienced in Thessalonica. Their faith was growing, their love was abounding, and their patience in tribulations was enduring. They are the church!

Much of what is presented here has been addressed in the commentary on 1 Thessalonians: faith, love, and patience (1:2-4), trials (3:1-5), abounding (4:1-2), and giving thanks (5:18). The interested reader should study those sections of the commentary to pursue these topics.

One helpful application of these verses is to note the continued faith of the Thessalonians in the midst of their various trials. These Christians were facing persecution, a reality generally unknown to American Christians. They also had several points of misunderstanding concerning the return of Christ that made some of them think they had missed Christ's return. But even with these obstacles, they continued in the faith, and for this, Paul was thankful. They have not turned away because of bad times, and they have not turned away because of bad theology. Their *faith* was "the substance of things hoped for, the evidence of things not seen" (Hebrews 11:1). Theirs was a concrete belief in a future, unseen truth. Their faith shaped their lives in the face of much uncertainty. May that be true of us as well.

3. Evidence of authentic judgment (1:5-10)

The growth in faith and love experienced by the Thessalonians was one indication that their faith was authentic. Paul's comments are rightly filled with praise.

Verses 5-10 show that increasing faith and love was not the only aspect of their authentic faith in Christ. That their faith was growing in the midst of persecution is further evidence that their faith was authentic.

If Christians are ever tempted to say that troubles are an indication of God's disapproval, Paul provides evidence to the contrary in these next verses. Besides affirming their faith, Paul also provides two positive and two negative aspects of authentic judgment.

(1:5) which is manifest evidence of the righteous judgment of God, that you may be counted worthy of the kingdom of God, for which you also suffer;

The persecution mentioned in 1 Thessalonians had continued. In verse 4, Paul said that their "patience and faith" in the midst of these "persecutions and tribulations" was evidence of their faith. Modern Christians may wonder what form this persecution took. Elias (in the *Believers Church Bible Commentary*, page 257) says that persecution likely came as political and civic suspicion. The government

116

of Rome did not look with favor on those who called anyone other than Caesar "Lord." Friends and neighbors of the Thessalonians looked with suspicion on those who did not participate in civic religion. Although the exact nature of the persecution directed toward these Christians is unknown, it likely came as punishment for breaking the law, and the loss of respect among other non-Christian citizens of the city.

The Thessalonians' choice to shape their decisions, their relationships, and their lifestyles according to the gospel of Jesus Christ gave those who were opposed to the gospel opportunity to make their lives difficult. In fact, if they had not been so faithful to the gospel, they would have avoided some persecution.

For those who ask "How do I know that I possess authentic Christian faith," persecution can be positive evidence of a faithful walk. Persecution is not the only indicator of authentic faith, however, and the absence of persecution does not mean a Christian is unfaithful. Persecution must be seen in its proper light.

To be "counted worthy" means simply that the Thessalonian Christians were saved. Their sins had been forgiven and God's favor was upon them, though they were suffering. Again, it is important that suffering is seen in its proper light. These believers were not counted worthy *because* they were suffering. They were counted worthy because they were *faithful*.

(1:6) since it is a righteous thing with God to repay with tribulation those who trouble you,

Because the persecution was likely causing questions about God and faith among church members, Paul gives an explanation of authentic judgment. Verse 6 is the first of two negative aspects of God's judgment, namely, that God will settle all accounts. It is part of God's righteous character that the unrighteous will be judged and punished for failing to respond to God's invitation. The theme of God's judgment is a consistent thread woven throughout the Scripture. Those who have caused suffering among believers will be repaid with "tribulation."

(1:7) and to give you who are troubled rest with us when the Lord Jesus is revealed from heaven with His mighty angels,

Paul continues with the first positive aspect of judgment. Those who are faithful will receive "rest" from their trouble. The future happiness of believers is often represented by the image of *rest*. The time of "rest" (and the judging of the unrighteous mentioned in verse 6) will occur in connection with the return of Jesus.

The "rest" described in verse 7 refers to being "always...with the Lord" (1 Thessalonians 4:17) and with the faithful saints ("with us"). This is a future promise that remains ever before the church. Trials and persecutions are not eternal for those who are faithful. Even if such trials extend the full length of their earthly lives, the unrighteous will be judged and repaid with "tribulation" and the righteous will rest in the very presence of our Lord Jesus.

(1:8-9) in flaming fire taking vengeance on those who do not know God, and on those who do not obey the gospel of our Lord Jesus Christ. These shall be punished with everlasting destruction from the presence of the Lord and from the glory of his power,

Paul continues the discussion of judgment by returning to the negative aspects of judgment. He repeats the theme of "tribulations" for those who are unrighteous by describing in more detail the type of punishment it will be. God's judgment against the unjust will consist of "flaming fire" and it will involve "everlasting destruction from the presence" of God.

People today often shun the notion of an eternal hell and the biblical descriptions of "fire" and suffering. The idea of Satan and hell is often portrayed in cartoon-fashion, with Satan dressed in a red suit with horns and a pitchfork. Hell is often described in equally comical terms.

Such portrayals miss the most important point of eternal punishment: suffering will be found in being eternally separated from God, knowing that ample opportunity had been given to follow Jesus. While some find the idea of Satan overseeing a hell of "flames" too much to believe, all would do well to consider the idea of being separated from that which God offers to them, and being totally given over to the just penalty for sin. Such a reality stands in stark contrast to God's promise in 1 Thessalonians 4:17, of "always [being] with the Lord."

(1:10) when He comes, in that Day, to be glorified in His saints and to be admired among all those who believe, because our testimony among you was believed.

This section concludes with the second positive aspect of judgment. All of the things mentioned above will be worked out on the day Jesus returns. Paul and his fellow missionaries provided a true explanation of the gospel and a testimony of the work of Jesus Christ. This testimony "was believed" by the Thessalonians, and in spite of hardship and suffering, they continued to prove the truth of their testimony. While their situation looked bleak, there was something to hold on to; they could joyfully look forward to "that Day," when the glory of their Savior will be revealed.

4. Prayer for continued faith (1:11-12)

Paul concludes his comments in this section by reporting on the missionaries' prayer for the Thessalonians.

(1:11-12) Therefore we also pray always for you that our God would count you worthy of this calling, and fulfill all the good pleasure of His goodness and the work of faith with power, that the name of our Lord Jesus Christ may be glorified in you, and you in Him, according to the grace of our God and the Lord Jesus Christ.

The two Thessalonian letters at times contain Paul's actual prayers. These verses, however, are not a prayer but a prayer report. Here Paul tells the Thessalonians how he has been praying for them. His joy is increased because he can see how God has been working through these prayers in very specific ways.

Paul's prayers have consisted of requests to God that the Thessalonians would live an authentic faith, and that God would be glorified through their living. Paul has commented often on how these specific prayer requests have been realized in their lives.

It is always good to know that people are praying for us. No matter what our circumstances are, the knowledge that others are remembering us in prayer is a wonderful blessing. Paul knew that his teaching and encouraging ministry was only part of his work among the Thessalonians. Prayer was essential.

There are times when it is also helpful to know how we are being prayed for. It is appropriate in these times to give people specific items to include in their prayers for us. Paul's prayer report in verses 11-12 is an excellent model of how we can encourage one another and grow in faith. We are to pray for one another, but we are also to let people know the content of our prayers, that we might encourage one another, as well as pray more effectively.

Chapter 8

FURTHER TEACHING ON THE
RETURN OF CHRIST
2 Thessalonians 2:1-17

Second Thessalonians 2 is a significant portion of the letter, in that the topic of Jesus' return is the single largest topic in the letter. The topic of Christ's return has already been taken up in 1 Thessalonians 4:13—5:11. In those verses, the emphasis is on the future of believers who have died before Christ's return (4:13-18), and the suddenness of their Lord's return (5:1-11).

A quick analysis of 2 Thessalonians 2 indicates that here there is a different focus for writing about the return of Christ. In this chapter, the focus is on the signs that will precede the *parousia* (the coming), and what will happen to those persons who do not acknowledge Jesus as Savior (before the final judgment). Even though the return of Christ will be as sudden as "a thief in the night," Paul indicates that there will be indications that the time is close. There will be need for extra vigilance.

One significant point in the material presented in this chapter is that, for the Thessalonians, this is not new teaching. Paul taught the church about Christ's return when he was with them, as his comment in verse 5 indicates: "Do you remember that when I was still with you I told you these things?" While "these things" certainly were part of his teaching in Thessalonica, he does not repeat them here. The identity of "these things" is in places uncertain. Interpretation will call for a measure of humility in such times.

Even if there will be a point or two which will be left somewhat open-ended, Christians will find much in these verses in which to place significant hope. Regardless of the nature and character of the forces that will oppose Christ, the salvation of the Christian is well grounded in the present and future work of God.

1. Clearing up misinformation (2:1-2)

This chapter begins with Paul setting the minds of the Thessalonian congregation at ease over some misinterpreted or possibly even false information which has been causing considerable confusion and distress in the church.

(2:1-2) Now, brethren, concerning the coming of our Lord Jesus Christ and our gathering together to Him, we ask you, not to be soon shaken in mind or troubled, either by spirit or by word or by letter, as if from us, as though the day of Christ had come.

The study of 1 Thessalonians showed that these Christians were extremely interested in the return of Christ. In fact, one might wonder if they were not *too* interested in Christ's return, in that they were easily saddened or confused over the timing of His return, and that certain ones of the congregation had apparently stopped working to await Christ's return (the topic of chapter 3).

Whatever the case, this is now the second time Paul has had to provide teaching concerning the return of Christ. This time, however, something had happened to cause the Thessalonians confusion; they came to believe that the rapture had happened, and they had missed it. Because Paul was still separated from the Thessalonians by many miles, it was not completely clear to him what the source of the confusion might be. He offers several possibilities. First, it may have been *by spirit*, perhaps indicating a word of (false) prophecy which had been delivered in a worship service. Second, it may have been *a word*, which suggests some teaching going on in the congregation by someone who had misunderstood what Paul wrote in his earlier letter. Finally (and most disturbing), it may have been *by letter, as if from us*. Possibly there existed a forger who had written to the Thessalonians in Paul's name, offering them this false teaching.

If Paul could not be certain what the source of mis-information was, it is certainly not possible for modern readers to know, either. The best clue as to Paul's thinking may be found in 3:17, where he says, "The salutation of Paul with my own hand, which is a sign in every epistle; so I write." It was Paul's practice to dictate his letters, but in several of them (1 Corinthians, Galatians, Colossians, and Philemon) he mentions that he is personally signing them. The ending of this letter does seem to make a point other than to just say "good-bye," as if Paul wants to assure the Thessalonians that this letter is indeed his. The content is trustworthy.

Whatever the source of confusion, Paul's words that followed are intended to straighten things out. They need not be *shaken in mind* or *troubled*. As we will see below, not only has the day of Christ not yet arrived, the signs which indicate His coming have not even occurred. To paraphrase Winston Churchill, this is not the end—it is not even the beginning of the end.

2. Signs of the return of Christ (2:3-12)

Having addressed the source of confusion (whatever it may have been), Paul now turns his attention to outlining some of the events which will precede the return of Christ, events that Paul had presumably already shared with the Thessalonians.

Like many New Testament passages which address

the end times, Paul offers signs which are to be looked for. It is tempting to read passages such as this one and attempt to say what these signs will actually be like when they happen. While Paul does talk about many specific things that will happen, some restraint must be shown in attempting to describe these signs. The signs that are provided are given in a general fashion—what they will actually look like when they occur is not stated. For those who are concerned that they will the miss signs, Paul will later say that only those who do not follow Christ in the first place will be deluded. Those who are Christians, and who have an awareness of what is to come, can take hope in that when the signs occur, they will know them!

(2:3-4) Let no one deceive you by any means; for that Day will not come unless the falling away comes first, and the man of sin is revealed, the son of perdition, who opposes and exalts himself above all that is called God or that is worshiped, so that he sits as God in the temple of God, showing himself that he is God.

Christians need to exercise due diligence in matters of the end times, so that they will not be deceived. One might wonder if, in fact, Paul felt the Thessalonians had been deceived. This is a common question believers today have as well. From the comments in this chapter, it seems likely to say that the Thessalonians were *confused*. They clearly were not reflecting an adequate understanding of Christ's return. The word *deceived* refers to those persons who will not believe the signs even when they are actually occurring. Paul will later say that such persons are non-believers.

The first sign Paul gives concerns the falling away. Careful attention to the text shows that this "falling away" is a specific event or time period—it is named "the" falling away. It should also be noted that the falling away is not an event which describes the world in general, or even non-believers specifically. Such persons who have no faith in Christ have nothing from which to fall away. This is an event which describes the church.

Both of these points must be considered carefully. It is easy to lament declining morality in the world, and sadly, in the church, and equate such times with events like these. Similarly, there have been times in the history of the church when believers have fallen away under threat or actual experience of persecution. Still, neither of these general realities should be attributed to the specific event described in 2 Thessalonians 2:3.

"The falling away" refers to a specific time when some, perhaps many, Christians will fall away from Christ and the church because of the great persecution which will be released in the end times. It is natural for concerned Christians to wonder what this time will be like. Such questions rise out of a natural curiosity about the end times, and often come from a desire similar to that of the Thessalonians—a desire not to miss the return of Christ.

Such interest is legitimate. On this point, however, we must admit that we do not know *exactly* how such events will transpire. But that is not to say that we know nothing of what will happen. Paul is not the only New Testament writer to make reference to end time events. Concerning "the falling away," Jesus himself referred to just such an event while teaching about the signs of the end of the age in the synoptic Gospels.[38] Matthew 24:9-13 describes the time of the falling away as a time of great persecution against the church, where believers will be persecuted and martyred. Those that

---

[38] See Matthew 24:1-51; Mark 13:1-37; Luke 21:5-17. In the interest of space and clarity, primary attention will be given to the account in Matthew; other gospels will be used as needed.

"turn away" from the church and from believing the truth of God's Word, will betray Christians to the authorities. How this will come about on a large scale is impossible to speculate. One can only assume that it will be recognized for what it is when the time arrives.

In addition to "the falling away," another sign of the end times is the revealing of the "man of sin" or "son of perdition."[39] In describing this future person, Paul uses the Greek word *anomia* (here translated "sin") which means "wicked" or "lawless." "Perdition" translates the Greek word *apoleias*, which means "destruction, ruin, waste."

As with the falling away, this *man of sin* is referred to in other portions of the New Testament as well. He is described as "the Antichrist" in 1 John 2:18. In the Revelation, John refers to this person symbolically as "the beast rising out of the sea." (Revelation 13:1-10).

What is most significant about this person is that he will oppose things of God, even going so far as to sitting in the temple of God, proclaiming to be God. How will this person be able to claim to be God? He will presumably do it through the working of "power, signs, and lying wonders," described below in verse 9. Bible students express a variety of opinions as to how this person will sit in the temple of God, since the temple was destroyed in the year 70 A.D. It could be that another temple is yet to be built. It may also be that Paul is speaking symbolically here, and that the reference to the temple is meant to represent how the man of sin will stand against all that is holy and right.

So it is that the end times will begin. Such events, according to Paul, will occur before the rapture and the "day

---

[39]   The word "first" in verse 3 is best understood as referring to both of these events happening somewhat simultaneously, in the sense that these events mark the beginning.

of the Lord." The events will be so severe that even some in the church will turn away—either because their hearts turn against God, or because they are deceived by the work of the "man of sin."

(2:5) Do you not remember that when I was still with you I told you these things?

It is at this point in the letter where some caution must begin to be exercised in the interpretation. Clearly, what is provided in these verses is a "refresher" for the Thessalonians. They have heard this before, and Paul is providing an outline of what he had taught them to calm their worries that they had missed the return of the Lord.

The challenge for modern interpreters is that Paul does not include in his letter everything that he taught them when he "was still with" them. There are some points on what is being presented here, where we may assume the Thessalonians knew more than we do. Present day readers must realize that only the Thessalonian congregation would be able to fully "remember" what had been taught.

(2:6-7) And now you know what is restraining, that he may be revealed in his own time. For the mystery of lawlessness is already at work; only He who now restrains will do so until He is taken out of the way.

Second Thessalonians 2:6-7 are widely considered some of the most difficult verses in the New Testament. As a way of appreciating the challenges of these two verses, one only has to think of the last time he undertook a household repair job that appeared simple at first, but eventually required three trips to the hardware store to fix both the initial project and the two other items that needed fixing once the initial project was undertaken. At least in the beginning, the more one looks at these two verses, the more complex they become. Because of the unique challenges these verses present, a broader range of information and depth of detail is provided than in other sections of the commentary. The added detail will be helpful for readers who are studying other commentaries along with this one.

The reasons for the difficulties are two-fold. The first reason was mentioned in the commentary on verse 5 above: modern readers are not privileged to know everything Paul taught in Thessalonica.

The second difficulty deals with the identity of the one restraining the "man of sin." What and who is doing the restraining? Is it a power? A spiritual being? A political institution? Adding to the challenge of identifying the re-strainer is the grammar of the Greek text, which clearly re-fers to the identity of the restrainer in two ways: both as a force or institution (*what is restraining*, verse 6), and a per-son (*He who now restrains*, verse 7).[39] Providing a clear, non-controversial identity to the restrainer has proved to be a difficult question, one that biblical scholars have been de-bating for many hundreds of years. Even the church father Augustine admitted that some of what is mentioned here simply can not be known with certainty.[40]

Scholars come down in one of two camps on the identity of the one doing the restraining. Some suggest that the restrainer is a force of good. The NKJV suggests that it is God doing the restraining, by saying "He who now re-

---

[39] The reference in verse 6 in the Greek text is a neuter participle. The neuter gender in the Greek language is used to refer to "impersonal" objects in a general sort of way (such as a generic reference to "the government"). The reference in verse 7 is a masculine participle. The masculine (or feminine) gender in the Greek language is used to refer to persons or specific objects (such as a specific reference to "The President"). The challenge in these verses is to name some-thing that can be referred to both in a general and specific sense.

[40] Michael Holmes, *1 & 2 Thessalonians, NIV Application Commentary*, page 234.

strains."

An opposite understanding says that some force of evil, either Satan himself or the Roman government, is doing the restraining of evil, until the "time is right" for Satan to launch his final, all-out attack against God. Such an interpretation explains why Paul is so vague in his references on this point. He could not risk being too specific in writing lest his letter is intercepted by the authorities, causing further trouble for the Thessalonians.

The difficulties with this line of interpretation, however, are two-fold. First, if Satan is the restrainer, then it would appear Satan is divided against himself: why should Satan hold back his own agent? Second, if the Roman government is the restrainer, then why has Christ not returned now that the Roman government has been "out of the way" for more than 1,500 years?

The position of this commentary is that the restraining force is a force of good. It is, in fact, the Holy Spirit. Two reasons are given for this interpretation.

1. Continuing the technical point of grammar from earlier, John's gospel refers to the Holy Spirit both in the general sense as a "power" and as a specific person. Since it is correct to refer to the Holy Spirit in both senses, identifying the restrainer as the Holy Spirit fits Paul's choice of grammar.[41]

2. Identifying the restrainer as the Holy Spirit makes it clear that God is in control of all of life's events, a general point Paul makes clear in this passage. There will be times in world history where it *appears* Satan is in control. There will even be periods where God *allows* Satan a measure of con-

---

[41]   See John 14:16-17. The name "Helper" is masculine. The name "Spirit" is neuter.

trol. But when "the trumpet of God" sounds (1 Thessalonians 5:16), God will quite easily regain the control that has rightly been His all along.

It is important to not get so consumed on this point of uncertainty that the greater point is missed. However evil the present age is, or will become, it will be worse in the end times. Once the restraining work is complete, this man of sin, whose identity has long been an object of speculation, will be revealed. Such is the topic of the next verses.

(2:8-10) And then the lawless one will be revealed, whom the Lord will consume with the breath of His mouth and destroy with the brightness of His coming. The coming of the lawless one is according to the working of Satan, with all power, signs, and lying wonders, and with all unrighteous deception among those who perish, because they did not receive the love of the truth, that they might be saved.

After this "lawless one" is revealed, this person will have a period of time to work "with all power, signs and lying wonders." The stage will be set for the manifestation of wickedness in all of its ghastly forms, but this evil person will eventually be destroyed by Christ when He comes in all His glory (verse 8b). God is sovereign, even over the activities of the evil powers.

During the time the lawless one is allowed to work, many non-believers will perish due to the lying wonders of this person. What will appear to be of God will be proved in the end to be the work of Satan, and many will die eternally because of their own choices (verse 10).

Many persons do not like to hear of such a future. And yet for those who refuse God's invitation to salvation, and will not "receive the love of the truth, that they might be saved," there will be no way to distinguish the works of Satan apart from the works of God. The inner testimony of the Holy Spirit will not be present to enable one to know the truth. Such persons will receive the logical consequence of their own choice against God.

(2:11-12) And for this reason God will send them strong delusion, that they should believe the lie, that they all may be condemned who did not believe the truth but had pleasure in unrighteousness.

Throughout the Bible, God's judgment comes as the logical consequence of sinful choices. When people turn their backs on God and continue in sin, then judgment follows as the consequence of those decisions. In the short term, this judgment is found in earthly consequences of such choices: for example, adultery leads to divorce and broken homes; stealing leads to a lack of trust, even time in jail.

Verse 11 continues the thought of verse 10. The Greek for "will send" is actually in the present tense; a better translation of this verse is "And for this reason God sends them strong delusion." The delusion is the consequence of refusing to "receive the love of the truth" and believing that the works of evil are better than the works of God. Those who have "pleasure in unrighteousness" will be condemned.

3. Hope for the believer (2:13-17)

Throughout this chapter, Paul has been addressing a primary concern of the Thessalonians—that they had somehow missed the return of the Lord. But through the entire discussion, the implication has been clear: the Lord has not returned, but when He does, many will suffer for their lack of faith in the Lord Jesus Christ.

Having provided this clarification, Paul now turns the discussion completely around with what must have been joyous news to the Thessalonians. What has just been discussed does not apply to you! Paul has been outlining the fate of non-believers. Now he turns his attention to the Thessalonians, and their standing before Christ.

(2:13-14) But we are bound to give thanks to God always for you, brethren beloved by the Lord, because God from the beginning chose you for salvation through sanctification by the Spirit and belief in the truth, to which He called you by our gospel, for the obtaining of the glory of our Lord Jesus Christ.

The doctrine of election has been discussed in the commentary on 1 Thessalonians 1:4. Here, however, Paul adds two important aspects of the salvation of the believer; salvation involves both *living* (sanctification by the Spirit) and *believing* (belief in the truth).

Often times Christians tend to emphasize one of these aspects of salvation over the other. There are those believers who tend to emphasize salvation as a manner of living. For these Christians, true believers are identified by the quality of their works. The depth of their faith will be measured in how they act toward "the least of these." Christians who emphasize the "living" side of salvation are often interested in social justice types of ministries—peace, social action, and the like. Doctrine is not ignored, but is not the primary emphasis of these persons.

On the other end of the spectrum are those Christians who emphasize "believing." They are more interested in understanding the doctrines of the church and making certain that others in their congregations are people of strong faith in the basic tenets of Scripture. For these Christians, true believers are identified by their upholding certain theological understandings. Social action is not ignored by such believers, but the emphasis tends to be on evangelism and proper belief, more than on social action.

Admittedly, these descriptions are generalizations.

Yet one does not have to look very far in the church to see how this is true. "Service" and "evangelism" are too often separated in the church's ministries. Whether one uses the words "liberal," "social gospel," "conservative," or "evangelical," the broad categories of emphasis are easily seen in the church. Christians tend to emphasize either "living," or "believing," often at the expense of the other.

But in these verses, Paul links together these two aspects of salvation. They are both a natural outflow of salvation. When persons are "sanctified," a radical change begins in the lives of individuals, and they are literally changed into new beings. There is no way that this change can be hidden, and the life—the "living"—of the believer will be different.

Belief is also important. One cannot simply choose what to believe or what is believable. The Scripture and Christian tradition are two of the tools that the Holy Spirit uses to bring this sanctification into reality. To ignore either of these is to miss a vital aspect of the Christian faith. Brethren pastor, Galen Hackman, illustrates this point well when he writes: "Our mission is to share the gospel. This remains the Great Commission of the church. Doing this effectively with a concern for the whole person will often include the compassionate care of physical needs. But the church's mission should never stop at that, nor should it separate its compassion from its evangelism."[42]

(2:15) Therefore, brethren, stand fast and hold the traditions which you were taught, whether by word or our epistle.

The word "traditions" refers to the handing down of knowledge, beliefs, and customs from the past—deeply rooted so that they become a kind of rule of life. Traditions

---

[42]   Galen Hackman, *Evangelism and Service*, Brethren Press, page 26.

can be *good* ("stand fast and hold the traditions," as specified here in 2 Thessalonians 2:15); they can be *useless* ("aimless conduct received by tradition from your fathers," as noted in 1 Peter 1:18); or *evil* ("you hold the tradition of men," as pointed out in Mark 7:8).

The word "traditions" is used in a wholesome sense in 2 Thessalonians 2:15, but if the tradition is such that it undermines a command of God, then believers are better off dispensing with the tradition. Jesus reprimanded the Pharisees: "For laying aside the commandment of God, you hold the tradition of men—the washing of pitchers and cups, and many other such things you do" (Mark 7:8).

For the congregation at Thessalonica which was struggling in its beliefs about the day of the Lord, as well in some areas of living (as discussed at various points throughout the commentary), the admonition to "stand fast and hold the traditions which you were taught," may well be the most important instruction found in either letter.

The keeping of this verse is in many ways the heritage of many Anabaptist and Pietist congregations. It has been said of the Church of the Brethren that "the primary impulse of the early Brethren was to restore the primitive Apostolic Church. Their ideal was to return the church to the exact condition in which Jesus had left it, or, as they were wont to say, of 'earnestly contending for the faith once delivered to the saints.'"[43] As can be seen in the historical records of both Mennonite and Brethren church meetings, much attention was given to maintaining the traditions as they were done in the beginning. "Innovations" (new practices or beliefs) were typically rejected, either because they could not be supported by Scripture, or because they were out of order with

---

[43]   Carl Bowman, *Brethren Society*, page 26.

the tradition of the church body.

It is the strength of the church to hold the traditions which it was taught. The moral fabric of our society is being stretched and challenged at a rate unheard of in the history of the world. What is even more unsettling is the rate at which Christians find their time occupied by activities outside the church, to the point where church functions must be "fit in" around other schedules. Even then attendance and participation is not what it used to be or ought to be. There is little wonder why believers are uncertain about their beliefs. It is their traditions which help believers remain well rooted in the ever-shifting moral landscape of this world. Before people get frustrated with their own church tradition and go looking for another, they would do well to make sure they understand and live those traditions in a deeper fashion, trusting that the Spirit will lead them to depths of understanding which will nourish their soul in ways they have not yet imagined.

(2:16-17) Now may our Lord Jesus Christ Himself, and our God and Father, who has loved us and given us everlasting consolation and good hope by grace, comfort your hearts and establish you in every good word and work.

Paul included a special blessing for the Christians at Thessalonica. The blessing is specific to the situation it addresses. The Thessalonians had been "shaken in mind," fearing they had missed the return of the Lord. Paul wishes them to know "everlasting consolation and good hope" now that they have been properly informed. They are not to be troubled or upset. Instead, they are to know comfort and be "established in every good word and work."

Knowing that the Lord Jesus Christ has control of the future should provide comfort and hope amid the challenges and struggles of life. To believers who diligently pursue an ongoing relationship with Him—a relationship that is expressed through living and believing, and is carried out in fellowship with others in the church—grace will be given to provide strength that will sustain them well. Christians may not know the answer to every challenge, but a Christian knows where to turn for the answer. Trials and difficulties need not overcome believers who are firmly rooted in their relationship with the Lord.

Chapter 9

FURTHER EXHORTATION TO
SPIRITUAL DILIGENCE
2 Thessalonians 3:1-18

As Paul concludes this second letter to the Thessalonians, he includes many comments that are similar to what has come before. He asks to be remembered in prayer, as the work of evangelism and church planting is a challenging one. He addresses the continuing problem of certain ones among them refusing to work. Finally, he gives the standard closing to letters.

In all of this, Paul, Silvanus, and Timothy wish to exhort the Thessalonians to diligence in prayer and practice that the word of the Lord may continue to do its good work.

1. Diligence in prayer (3:1-2)

Instruction on prayer has not been a significant topic in either of these letters. The only general principle given on the topic of prayer was found in 1 Thessalonians 5:17, where Paul instructed the Thessalonians to "pray without ceasing." Instead of addressing the topic of prayer head on, Paul has kept prayer near the surface throughout each of the two letters, quietly suggesting a model for living rather than giving explicit teaching. At times, the letters themselves have seemed to be prayers.

As Christians, it is good to have "refresher courses" on the topic of prayer. Christians ought to always be brushing up their prayer skills. What is most telling, however, is the life of the believer that is obviously characterized by much prayer, even if not much is directly said about prayer. Such a commitment to prayer will make a significant difference in the life of the believer. Clearly, this is the life Paul lived, and it is how he wants the Thessalonians to live as well.

(3:1-2) Finally, brethren, pray for us, that the word of the Lord may run swiftly and be glorified, just as it is with you, and that we may be delivered from unreasonable and wicked men; for not all have faith.

1. Prayer for the missionaries. As he did in 1 Thessalonians 5:25, Paul requests again that the Thessalonians remember him, Silvanus, and Timothy in prayer. The reasons are quite specific and common sense. In evangelism and church planting work, much contact will necessarily be with persons who are not believers. These may be unsaved persons with whom the evangelist is sharing the gospel. It may be with government officials who are hostile to the gospel. In the modern context, it may be with zoning boards and building inspectors, but most of all with people in the community, as believers seek to bring others to faith in Christ. Such persons can sometimes be "unreasonable and wicked" if they choose to be.

When the evangelistic effort is sufficiently bathed in prayer, such obstacles have been known to "disappear" due to the blessing of the Lord. It is always an opportunity for praise and thanksgiving when opportunities to share the gospel are found in abundance and go well. At such times, it can truly be said that the "word of the Lord" is "running swiftly" or having "free course" (as the KJV says).

The local church would do well to keep the congregation informed of such opportunities for prayer through prayer lists, bulletin boards, and prayer services. All who are in the front-line work of evangelism and church planting need the prayer support of the faithful congregation.

2. The result of prayer in the life of the congregation. The Thessalonians were waiting for the result of such prayers in their own lives. As they faced challenges of persecution from outside the congregation, and some struggles of belief and practice from within, they needed encouragement so that what they wished to accomplish would be their experience.

No matter how much emphasis is given to the ministry of the Spirit in the work of sanctification, the fact remains that spiritual transformation is hard work. The things of this world are a constant temptation to the Christian. It is easy to get frustrated, thinking that we are unable to live as the Lord directs in His Word. But in the pursuit of holiness in the life of the church, the Christian must not lose heart. Prayer will not only help win life's battles, it will also provide strength for the battles. As someone once said, prayer is not preparation for the battle, prayer is the battle.

In our local congregations, we would do well to consider what ministries are being undertaken that are so challenging, that church members are compelled to pray that God's will would be done. In the North American context, churches can accomplish much due to an abundance of resources and the general respect the church has in our society. While this is a blessing, such realities can also numb Christians into thinking that everything can be done in *our* strength, without dependence on the Spirit. It can also tempt us to think that any struggle or difficulty is an indication that something is *not* God's will, rather than the assurance that it *is* God's will. Every congregation would do well to undertake ministries so large that they force the congregation into new depths of prayer and worship.

2. Diligence in obedience (3:3-5)

Prayer is one essential quality in the life of a Christian. A second important quality is that of obedience—the

Christian faithfully doing the things God commands him to do. For Paul, obedience is always the second part of a two-step process in the relationship between God and Christians. First, God works in the life of the believer, calling the person into relationship with Him. Second, the believer responds to God out of obedience. Paul briefly touches on this relationship in verses 3-5.[44]

(3:3-5) But the Lord is faithful, who will establish you and guard you from the evil one. And we have confidence in the Lord concerning you, both that you do and will do the things we command you. Now may the Lord direct your hearts into the love of God and into the patience of Christ.

1. God's work in the Christian. In this brief section, Paul affirms once again that the Lord is *faithful*, something he affirmed in 1 Thessalonians 5:24. An aspect of the faithfulness of the Lord is that the Christian can count on being *established.* The idea of being established is an important one that shows up in many areas of life, not only one's spiritual life. The purpose of being established is that one might be better prepared for coming challenges.

Many persons will understand the idea of being established from gardening. Many gardeners will begin growing their plants indoors under a heat lamp, so the roots can be established and strengthened before the plant is transplanted to the outdoor garden, where it will face a variety of weather. If a plant is placed outdoors too soon, it may not have sufficient strength to survive the challenges of weather.

Likewise the Christian must depend on being established by the Lord that he might survive life's challenges. Jesus addresses this very need in the parable of the sower,

---

[44]   For more on the topic of obedience, see the BNTC Commentary on 1 Thessalonians 4:1-12.

when he says, "some [seed] fell on stony places, where they did not have much earth: and they immediately sprang up because they had no depth of earth. But when the sun was up they were scorched, and because they had no root they withered away" (Matthew 13:5-6). Jesus went on to explain that the sun represents "tribulation or persecution...because of the word" (Matthew 13:21).

Many new Christians face similar challenges as they separate from old, sinful ways of living, but even mature Christians are not immune to challenges, and must trust that God will establish them to face such challenges of living. Such establishing (mentioned three times prior to this in these epistles)[45] is for their spiritual benefit.

2. The Christian's response to God. In addition to being established, Paul desires that the Thessalonians obey the things they have been commanded. Such obedience was addressed in the commentary on 1 Thessalonians 4:1-12. Briefly put, the purpose of obedience is the demonstration of a faithful response to God. God desires our obedience as evidence of our faith and commitment to God's ways and to His plans for our lives.

3. A wish for deeper relationships of love. Paul concludes this section with a wish for the Thessalonians, that the Lord would direct their lives into the love of God and patience of Christ. As always, Paul recognizes that it is God who is the source of life of the Christians. Not only does God bless and provide for His children, God directs all their paths into closer relationship with Him. God's blessing through establishing believers, and the faithful response of obedience, will lead those who seriously follow Christ into a deep relationship of love and patience, both of which God eagerly

---

[45]   First Thessalonians 3:2, 3:13; 2 Thessalonians 2:17.

seeks for those who call on His name.

3. Diligence in living and discipline (3:6-15)

Throughout First Thessalonians, an underlying concern was that certain ones in the church were "disorderly" in some fashion, perhaps because they felt the return of the Lord was imminent. This was the topic of 1 Thessalonians 4:11-12. Paul does not spell out the exact nature of the trouble at that point, but his further comments here do shed more light on the issue. The issue is that there were some in the Thessalonian congregation who were not working. To make the matter worse, they may have also been meddling in the lives of other believers. Instead of being "busy," they earned the title of being "busybodies" (2 Thessalonians 3:11). Paul turns his attention to this topic. In fact, addressing the issue of these busybodies is the second largest topic in 2 Thessalonians, at least in terms of the number of verses given to it.

The instructions given in these verses have to do with church discipline. In the Pietist and Anabaptist church traditions, there are many quality resources available which address church discipline. Some comments will be made on the topic of church discipline here; the interested reader will easily find an abundance of quality resources which address the topic at greater depth.

(3:6) But we command you, brethren, in the name of our Lord Jesus Christ, that you withdraw from every brother who walks disorderly and not according to the tradition which he received from us.

The challenge that Paul is addressing is the category of persons in the Thessalonian church who are "disorderly." Despite the existence of what seems to be a few clues in the text, it is not completely clear what specific behavior Paul is

142

addressing. Some have speculated that such persons are not working because they feel the return of the Lord to be imminent. Such persons may have felt "super-spiritual" and wanted to completely give themselves to preparing for the Lord's return. Others have felt that these persons thought they had already missed the Lord's return, and saw no purpose in working. Either of these understandings can be drawn from Paul's comments in verse 10 that those who "will not work" shall not eat. Some translations (NIV and NRSV, to name two) follow this understanding by translating the *ataktos* in verse 6 as "idle."

What leads some to question either of these interpretations, however, is that Paul never specifically identifies this as the issue, in spite of the fact that this topic and the topic of the Lord's return are the two major teachings of the epistles. For all of the attention Paul gives to the misunderstandings the Thessalonians had concerning the return of Christ, it seems likely that were this one of the problems, he would have said so.[46]

Others have looked at the Greek word *ataktos* and translated it as "disorderly" (NKJV) or "unruly." Paul's mention that they are not walking "according to the tradition which he received from us" suggests that he interpreted being disobedient to the apostolic teaching and the present leadership of the church as unruly. Such persons should not be considered "unruly" in the terms of being troublemakers, but rather, in the sense of having a rebellious spirit.

In the end, it is not possible to say with certainty what the exact issue was. It could be, however, that the problem is a combination of the two. It is clearly Paul's wish in these

---

[46]   It should be noted as a general rule, however, that arguments from silence are somewhat risky.

letters that the Thessalonian Christians (and, by extension, all Christians) wait patiently and expectantly for the Lord's return while working faithfully at their jobs, providing for the needs of the family, and building up a good reputation in the community. Those who flaunt this advice, either by not working when capable, or being disobedient to the apostolic teachings, are ignoring his clear teaching and causing significant disruption and difficulty for those who are obediently following Christ. In some manner these busybodies were disrupting the orderly functioning and ministry of the church, including the common meals that were a part of church worship. Such behavior should be stopped.

(3:7-9) For you yourselves know how you ought to follow us, for we were not disorderly among you; nor did we eat anyone's bread free of charge, but worked with labor and toil night and day, that we might not be a burden to any of you, not because we do not have authority, but to make ourselves an example of how you should follow us.

Having identified the problem, Paul now provides an example to strengthen his teaching. Having provided teaching on being an "imitator" of himself and other Christians, Paul applies that teaching to their particular situation.

While Paul, Silvanus, and Timothy were in Thessalonica, they were obedient to the teaching of the Lord, and they worked to earn their own living, even though they had the "authority" to expect payment from the Thessalonians.[47] Their reason for conducting themselves in this way was specifically to "make ourselves an example of how you should follow us." These new Christians needed an example of godly living. What they received was a model of living that showed that living for Christ happens in more ways than

---

[47] This passage is one properly used to justify the existence of a financially supported ministry. See the commentary on 1 Thessalonians 2:8-10.

in "Sunday morning" attitudes, but affects all aspects of life. Even secular work falls under the Lordship of Christ.

(3:10-15) For even when we were with you, we commanded you this: If anyone will not work, neither shall he eat. For we hear that there are some who walk among you in a disorderly manner, not working at all, but are busybodies. Now those who are such we command and exhort through our Lord Jesus Christ that they work in quietness and eat their own bread. But as for you, brethren, do not grow weary in doing good. And if anyone does not obey our word in this epistle, note that person and do not keep company with him, that he may be ashamed. Yet do not count him as an enemy, but admonish him as a brother.

The busybodies who were not working may have been "sponging" off of those who were expecting to eat at the fellowship meals of the church, even though they had not brought any food. They likely were able-bodied and capable of working, thus contributing to the common good of the church. If this is the case, Paul's teaching is not that such persons should be put out to starve; it is that they should be denied permission to eat at the fellowship meals.

Such action by the church would be a very strong statement concerning the nature of the busybodies' actions. By saying that "those who do not work will not eat," the church would be denying these persons the fellowship of the church. It is at this point that many present-day Christians would object. Surely, some say, the church should not deny any person the fellowship of the church. Some would object that this is not the "loving" thing to do. Others would say that it is not "our place to judge." However, to think this way, no activity, no matter how detrimental to the life of the church, would ever get addressed.

But those who would object to the type of admonishment addressed here misunderstand biblical admonish-

145

ment on three points. First, the proper application of biblical admonishment does not break fellowship in the church. Sinful action does. In the Thessalonian church, the actions of the busybodies had already damaged the fellowship of the church. Admonishment seeks to correct the problem and protect the spiritual integrity of the church. Alexander Mack said of the ban, "the ban is an essential and necessary part of the church of Christ...there can be no church of Christ without the ban. Otherwise, the devil and his leaven of wickedness would soon contaminate the good."[48]

Second, the proper application of the ban does not mean such people are enemies. In fact, the opposite is true. When sin rises to a level that it threatens the stability of Christian fellowship, such persons are to be admonished as "a brother." Jesus takes a similar approach to this question in Matthew 18 when the offending member is finally treated as a heathen and a tax collector, persons for whom Jesus showed a great depth of love. The ban can only be done from a position of love. In applying the ban in this manner, Menno Simons says "but this shall be done according to the ordering of the Spirit of God before the breaking of the bread, so that we may all in one spirit and in one love break and eat from one bread and drink from one cup."[49]

Third, the admonishment referred to here is reserved for those (hopefully rare) instances where the behavior of the believer threatens the fellowship of the entire church.[50] This was the situation in Thessalonica—the behavior of the busybodies was affecting the entire congregation.

---

[48] Mack, in Eberly, ed. *The Complete Writings of Alexander Mack*, page 33.
[49] Menno in Yoder. Jacob Elias in *1 & 2 Thessalonians: Believer's Church Bible Commentary*, page 334.
[50] Matthew 18:15-20 seems to best apply to those instances of sin which affect other individuals, although it would be best not to force this distinction too far.

It is safe to say that the overwhelming majority of Christian churches today do not exercise any level of church discipline. No matter how damaging and hurtful a person's behavior might be in the church, seemingly all behavior is tolerated.

Admittedly, it is difficult to apply church discipline in today's permissive society. Persons who are disciplined can all too often move their membership to another church in the community, and criticize the former church for being "unloving." May it be that God would grant each of us the courage to both apply and submit to the loving admonishment of faithful Christian friends, if ever our behavior threatens the fellowship of the entire congregation.

4. Concluding blessing (3:16-18)

These final verses constitute the concluding section of the standard letter writing format of the day. Second Thessalonians is interesting in that it seems to have a "double ending" although there is not much to be made of that point.

Much of what Paul says here has been said before, and the comments will be necessarily brief.

(3:16-18) Now may the Lord of peace Himself give you peace always in every way. The Lord be with you all. The salutation of Paul with my own hand, which is a sign in every epistle; so I write. The grace of our Lord Jesus Christ be with you all. Amen.

On the "Lord of peace," see the comments on 1 Thessalonians 5:23-24. As before, Paul wishes that believers would experience God's peace in every aspect of their living, confident that God is with the believer in all areas of life, no matter how difficult or trying.

Paul ends the letter by taking the pen from the scribe and including a few comments in his own handwriting.

Based on the comments of chapter 2, some might see this as evidence that Paul felt the Thessalonians had received a forged letter, and Paul wanted to authenticate this one with his own handwriting. While admitting that this might be an interpretation of this verse, this is not the only instance where Paul wrote a few comments with his own hand.[51]

Paul finally concludes what has been preserved of the Thessalonian correspondence with a benediction fitting for us all: The grace of our Lord Jesus Christ be with you all. Amen.

---

[51] See 1 Corinthians 16:21, Galatians 6:11, Colossians 4:18, and Philemon 1:19.

1. In what ways are you able to refer to God as our Father (or my Father)? How does addressing God in this more personal manner encourage your faith? (2 Thessalonians 1:1-2).

2. How have you maintained your faith in times of trouble, or in times where your understanding of God was incorrect? (2 Thessalonians 1:3-4).

3. What is the difference between being confused and being deceived on a matter of biblical doctrine? (2 Thessalonians 2:3-4)

4. Describe "the falling away" (2 Thessalonians 2:3-4). How will it differ from the present declining moral state of society?

5. What are the challenges in identifying the restrainer? (2 Thessalonians 2:6-7).

6. How well does your congregation balance social justice ministries and evangelistic ministries? (2 Thessalonians 2:13-14).

7. How does a congregation balance tradition and innovation? Are traditions always good, and should they always be continued? Should innovations always be avoided? (2 Thessalonians 2:15).

8. What types of "lying wonders" can you identify as present in our world today? (2 Thessalonians 2:8-10).

9. What ministries do you have in your local church that are a source of constant prayer? Is your local church undertaking anything so big that its success is not completely certain? What do such events do for our faith and prayer life? (2 Thessalonians 3:1-2).

10. How might struggle and difficulty indicate that a certain activity is God's will? (2 Thessalonians 3:1-2).

11. List both positive and negative aspects (and experiences) of church discipline. How can the church practice discipline in today's world in a manner that is redemptive? (2 Thessalonians 3:6-15).

SELECTED BIBLIOGRAPHY
1 and 2 Thessalonians

Augsburger, Myron S. *Quench Not the Spirit*. Scottdale, PA: Herald Press, 1975.

Barnes, Albert. *Barnes Notes on the New Testament: Thessalonians through Philemon*. Grand Rapids, MI: Baker Book House, 1961.

Bass, Dorothy C., ed. *Practicing Our Faith: A Way of Life for a Searching People*. San Francisco, CA: Josey-Bass Publishers, 1997.

Brother Lawrence. *The Practice of the Presence of God*. Pittsburgh, PA: Whitaker House, 1982.

Bowman, Carl F. *Brethren Society: The Cultural Transformation of a "Peculiar People."* Baltimore, MD: The Johns Hopkins University Press, 1995

Brown, Colin, ed. *New International Dictionary of New Testament Theology*, 4 volumes. Grand Rapids, MI: Zondervan, 1971.

Church of the Brethren home page, www.brethren.org.

Church of the Brethren Messenger, Elgin, IL: Brethren Press.

Durnbaugh, Donald F. *Fruit of the Vine*. Elgin, IL: Brethren Press, 1996.

Durnbaugh, Donald F. ed. *The Brethren Encyclopedia (3 Volumes)*. Elgin, IL: Brethren Press, 1983.

Eberly, William R. *The Complete Writings of Alexander Mack*. Winona Lake, IL: BMH Books, 1991.

Elias, Jacob W. *1&2 Thessalonians*. Scottdale, PA: Herald Press, 1995.

Fee, Gordon D. and Douglas Stuart. *How to Read the Bible for All Its Worth, 2nd Edition*. Grand Rapids, MI: Zondervan, 1993.

Foster, Richard J. *Prayer*. San Francisco, CA: Harper Collins, 1992.

Hackman, Galen. *Evangelism* and *Service*. Perspectives Essay Series. Elgin, IL: Brethren Press, 2001.

Harvey, Timothy. *To Judge or Not to Judge*. Perspectives Essay Series. Elgin, IL: Brethren Press, 2003.

Holmes, Michael W. *The NIV Application Commentary: 1 & 2 Thessalonians*. Grand Rapids, MI: Zondervan, 1998.

Hymnal: A Worship Book. Elgin, IL: Brethren Press, 1992.

Kreider, Alan. *The Change of Conversion and the Origin of Christendom: Christian Mission and Modern Culture*. Harrisburg, PA: Trinity Press International, 1999.

Limbaugh, David. *Persecution: How Liberals are Waging War Against Christianity*. Washington, DC: Regnery, 2003.

Martin, Harold S. *The Revelation*. Brethren New Testament Commentary. Ephrata, PA: Brethren Revival Fellowship, 2005.

Mennonite Church USA home page, www.mennoniteusa.org.

Morse, Kenneth I. *Preaching in a Tavern*. Elgin, IL: Brethren Press, 1997.

The Holy Bible, New International Version. Grand Rapids, MI: Zondervan, 1973.

Plunkett, Geraldine. *Nathan's Secret*. Elgin, IL: Brethren Press, 2000.

Shelly, John. "Dangers that Confront Preachers," in *BRF Witness*, Vol. 40, No. 2. Ephrata, PA, 2005.

Ulrich, Daniel & Janice Fairchild. *Caring Like Jesus: The Matthew 18 Project*. Elgin, IL: Brethren Press, 2002.

van Braght, Thieleman J. *The Bloody Theater or Martyrs Mirror of the Defenseless Christians*. Translated by Joseph F. Sohm. 3rd English Edition ed. Scottdale, PA: Herald Press, 1990.

VanGemeren, Willem A., ed. *New International Dictionary of Old Testament Theology and Exegesis*, 5 volumes. Grand Rapids, MI: Zondervan Publishing House, 1997.